SPECTRUM

Language Arts

Grade 5

Published by Spectrum
an imprint of Carson-Dellosa Publishing LLC
Greensboro, NC

Spectrum
An imprint of Carson-Dellosa Publishing LLC
P.O. Box 35665
Greensboro, NC 27425 USA

Printed in Kendallville, IN USA • All rights reserved.

ISBN 0-7696-5305-7

6 7 8 9 10 11 12 COU 13 12 11 10

335107780

Table of Contents Grade 5

Chapter 1 Grammar

Parts of Speech

Sentences

Table of Contents, continued

Table of Contents, continued

Chapter 1
Lesson 1.1 Common Nouns

Common nouns name people, places, and things. They are general nouns (not specific).

> *veterinarian* – a person
> A *veterinarian* is a doctor who helps animals.

> *city* – a place
> The *city* is in the southeastern part of the state.

> *shoe* – a thing
> My *shoe* is stuck in the mud.

Complete It
Use the words from the box below to complete the following sentences.

aunt	firefighters	park	sailors	trees
books	flowers	post office	telephone	track

1. The _____ look pretty in the vase.

2. The _____ rang and rang.

3. My _____ is visiting from Colorado.

4. The students run on the_____ beside the school.

5. _____ must not be afraid of smoke and fire.

6. The _____ is a nice place to play.

7. _____ on many subjects can be found in the library.

8. _____ must like living on the sea.

9. The _____ sells stamps.

10. Many _____ grow in this forrest.

Lesson 1.1 Common Nouns

Match It

Draw a line from Column A to Column B to match nouns. Practice it again by drawing lines from Column C to Column D.

Column A
person
place
thing

Column B
key
police officer
country

Column C
person
place
thing

Column D
student
gate
library

Try It

Write a short paragraph telling about a place you have visited. Use at least six common nouns.

_____

_____

_____

_____

_____

_____

_____

_____

_____

_____

Lesson 1.2 Proper Nouns

Proper nouns name specific people, places, and things. In a sentence, the noun is the person, place, or thing that can act or be talked about.

>*Dr. Bateman* – a specific person
>*Dr. Bateman* helped our sick puppy.
>
>*Anchorage* – a specific place
>*Anchorage* is a city in Alaska.
>
>*Empire State Building* – a specific thing
>The *Empire State Building* is in New York City.

Solve It
Write the correct words from the box to complete Patrick's journal entry. Use only proper nouns.

Uncle Rich	**Principal Ron**	**my principal**	**planet**
my school	**tomorrow**	**The Lord of the Rings**	**national park**
Grand Canyon	**Venus**	**the playground**	**my uncle**
book	**Saturday**	**Highland Park**	**Pierce School**

I love _____ mornings. I go to

_____ to walk the trails and read

_____. Later, Aunt Pat and

_____ come to my house. We plan

our trip to the _____. We use the

telescope to look at _____ when it

gets dark. On Monday, it's back to

_____. I like _____.

He is a good principal. But I still look forward to the

weekend.

Lesson 1.2 Proper Nouns

Find It
Use a dictionary to find at least 10 proper nouns. Remember, proper nouns always begin with a capital letter.

1. _____
2. _____
3. _____
4. _____
5. _____
6. _____
7. _____
8. _____
9. _____
10. _____

Try It
Use five proper nouns that you found in the dictionary to write a fictional paragraph. Also include common nouns in your paragraph.

_____

_____

_____

_____

_____

_____

_____

_____

_____

_____

_____

_____

_____

Lesson 1.3 Regular Plural Nouns

A **plural noun** names more than one person, place, or thing. Most nouns are made plural by adding an **s** to the end of the word.

  car**s**   cups   football**s**

Some nouns need an **es** added to the end of the word to make them plural. Nouns ending in the letters **s**, **x**, or **z** or in a **ch** or **sh** sound need **es**.

  boss**es**   tax**es**   waltz**es**   bench**es**   dish**es**

If a word ends in the letter **y**, then the **y** is changed to an **i** before adding the **es**.

  countr**ies**   cit**ies**   fl**ies**

However, words that end in **y** with a vowel before the **y** only add the **s**.

  boy**s**   key**s**   donkey**s**

In some cases, the noun has to change its spelling before making the plural form. If a noun ends in **f** or **fe**, and the **f** sound can still be heard in the plural form, just add **s**. However, if the final sound of the plural form is **v**, then change the **f** to **ve** and add the **s**.

  roof**s** (**f** sound)   gulf**s** (**f** sound)
  calv**es** (**v** sound)   loav**es** (**v** sound)

Identify It
Circle the correct spelling of the plural nouns in the following letter.

Dear Mom and Dad,

    Camp is great. I have made a lot of (friendes/friends). I have seen many (animals/animales). Two little (foxes/foxs) ran through the (woodes/woods) today. They are pretty. Tomorrow, we are going to hike. But don't worry, we won't go too close to the (cliffs/clives) or (valleyes/valleys). The (leaves/leafs) are falling here and turning color. One leaf is the color of the (cherrys/cherries) on our tree at home. I have to go now and help wash the dinner (dishes/dishs). After that, I have to practice for one of the (playes/plays). I miss you.

           Taylor

Lesson 1.3 Regular Plural Nouns

Solve It

Give an example for each of the rules below.

Rule: Nouns ending in the letters **s**, **x**, or **z** or in a **ch** or **sh** sound need **es**.

Example: _____

Rule: Words that end in **y** with a vowel before the **y** add **s**.

Example: _____

Rule: If a word ends in the letter **y**, then the **y** is changed to an **i** before adding the **es**.

Example: _____

Rule: If a noun ends in **f** or **fe**, and the **f** sound can still be heard in the plural form add **s**.

Example: _____

Try It

Make a list of ten of your favorite things. Then, on the lines next to them, write them in their plural form.

<u>singular</u>   <u>plural</u>

1. _____   _____

2. _____   _____

3. _____   _____

4. _____   _____

5. _____   _____

6. _____   _____

7. _____   _____

8. _____   _____

9. _____   _____

10. _____   _____

Lesson 1.4 Irregular Plural Nouns

Irregular plural nouns do not have a pattern for changing from singular to plural. These nouns and their plural spellings have to be learned.

Singular noun:	Plural noun:
child	children
man	men
woman	women

Some irregular nouns do not change at all when they are in the plural form. These forms also have to be learned.

Singular noun:	Plural noun:
cod	cod
rye	rye
wheat	wheat

The best way to learn these plural forms is by reading, writing, and practicing. Sometimes, when you read or hear these words used incorrectly, you will be able to tell if they are spelled incorrectly.

Complete It
Read the following paragraph. Choose the correct form of the irregular plural noun in the parentheses and write it on the line. Use a dictionary if you need help.

Hayley and Hannah love animals. They needed to do a project for school that

would help their community. They decided to do a project that would teach other

(children, childs) _____ about animals. They visited a wildlife center to get

information. They learned about (gooses, geese) _____, (deer, deers)

_____, and (mice, mouses) _____. They also learned

about different (fish, fishes) _____. They saw (cod, cods)

_____, (trouts, trout) _____, and (basses, bass)

_____. Hannah liked the (moose, mooses) _____ the best.

Hayley liked the (sheeps, sheep) _____. All of the children liked Hayley

and Hannah's report and wanted to visit and help the animals, too.

Lesson 1.4 Irregular Plural Nouns

Solve It
Find the following irregular plurals in the word search puzzle. The words can be forward, backward, vertical, horizontal, or diagonal.

bass	mice
children	moose
cod	rye
deer	sheep
fish	trout
geese	wheat
men	women

```
c  h  i  l  d  r  e  n  a  z
o  s  b  y  c  y  w  d  v  e
d  i  u  f  t  e  g  s  h  r
i  f  q  j  p  m  l  o  n  a
b  z  y  c  d  x  i  w  d  e
f  v  e  g  h  t  s  c  e  i
w  o  m  e  n  e  s  e  e  g
h  j  e  q  r  k  p  l  r  p
e  o  n  l  m  n  e  m  a  x
a  m  s  u  c  n  e  o  c  c
t  o  h  t  t  k  h  r  i  i
e  i  r  u  n  e  s  o  o  m
g  d  o  r  e  e  b  s  g  b
i  r  e  d  r  a  w  j  a  m
t  t  n  t  c  a  h  s  i  b
```

Try It
Choose five singular nouns and write their plural forms. Remember, these are all irregular plural nouns. Use a dictionary if you need help.

singular noun   plural noun

1. _____   _____

2. _____   _____

3. _____   _____

4. _____   _____

5. _____   _____

Lesson 1.5　Subject Pronouns

A **pronoun** is a word used in place of a noun. Pronouns can make writing and speaking more interesting. **Subject pronouns** are pronouns that replace the subject of the sentence.

> Pancakes are great for breakfast. Pancakes taste good with syrup.
> Pancakes are great for breakfast. *They* taste good with syrup.

In the example above, the pronoun *they* is a substitute for the noun *pancakes*.

Singular subject pronouns:	Plural subject pronouns:
I, you, he, she, it	we, you, they

Singular subject nouns:	Singular subject pronouns:
Debbie likes cats.	I like cats.
Lynn likes to run.	You like to run.
Ed works for a newspaper.	He works for a newspaper.
Carol is a teacher.	She is a teacher.
Bicycling is their favorite sport.	It is their favorite sport.

Plural subject nouns:	Plural subject pronouns:
Greg and Cliff are brothers.	We are brothers.
Lisa and Claudia are friends.	You are friends.
Jennifer and Julie are tennis partners.	They are tennis partners.

Match It

Match the following pronouns with the nouns they could replace. Write the correct answer or answers to Column A in Column B. There may be more than one correct answer.

I	he	it	
you	she	we	they

Column A	Column B
Jack and Jennifer	_____
Nicole	_____
ball	_____
Josh	_____
cars	_____

Lesson 1.5 Subject Pronouns

Complete It
Choose a subject pronoun to complete the following
passage. Each word may be used more than once.

I you	he she	it we	they

"Chris, are _____ awake?" Mrs. Johnson called from downstairs.

"_____ can't find my shoes. Do _____ know where

_____ are?" Chris shouted.

"Ask your sister. Maybe _____ has seen them." answered Mrs.

Johnson.

Chris knocked on Kendra's door. "Have _____ seen my shoes?

"_____ saw one earlier. _____ was in the dog's

mouth," Kendra replied.

"Mom, where's Toby?" Chris scrambled downstairs. "_____ am

going to be late for school!"

Mr. Johnson answered. "Toby's out back, and it looks like that little guy is digging a

hole. Wait, _____ is definitely covering something up.

_____ better get out there!"

Try It
Continue the story above using all of the subject pronouns from the box.

_____

_____

_____

_____

_____

_____

_____

Lesson 1.6 Object Pronouns

A **pronoun** is a word used in place of a noun. Pronouns can make writing and speaking more interesting. An **object pronoun** replaces the noun that is the receiver of the action in the sentence.

> Mrs. Johnson cooked dinner for Mr. Johnson.
> Mrs. Johnson cooked dinner for *him*.

In this example, the object pronoun *him* is a substitute for the object noun *Mr. Johnson*.

<u>Singular object pronouns:</u>

me	Mom cooked dinner for me.
you	Mom cooked dinner for you.
him	Mom cooked dinner for him.
her	Mom cooked dinner for her.
it	Mom cooked it.

<u>Plural object pronouns:</u>

us	Mom cooked dinner for us.
you	Mom cooked dinner for you.
them	Mom cooked dinner for them.

Identify It

Circle the errors in object pronoun use in the following school note. Write the correct object pronoun above the mistake. Not all object pronouns used in this note are mistakes.

The fifth-grade class at Riverview Elementary School is taking a field trip to the Science Museum on Wednesday, February 9. Your child has a permission slip. Please sign her. Return it to you by Friday, February 4. Principal Ann will be checking them. I will give them to it. Please fill in your child's name on the nametag and return it to you. Mr. Baum, the director of the Science Museum, will be checking it. I will give the tags to me. Your child will write a report about the visit. I will read you. I will also give him to you to read. Principal Ann and I will post the reports in the school. Please return them to them.

Thank you,

Mrs. Jones

Lesson 1.6 Object Pronouns

Rewrite It
Rewrite the following sentences. Replace the underlined object nouns with object pronouns.

1. I needed a pencil. Paul gave his pencil to <u>I</u>.

   _____

   _____

2. My cousin and I wanted to go the movies. Dad drove <u>my cousin and I</u>.

   _____

   _____

3. Tom drew a picture for his big brother, Brian. Tom likes drawing pictures for <u>Brian</u>.

   _____

   _____

4. Cathy and Marie won the game. The trophy goes to <u>Cathy and Marie</u>.

   _____

   _____

5. Michelle cooked dinner for her roommate, Jill. Michelle is a good cook and likes to cook for <u>Jill</u>.

   _____

   _____

6. Michelle cooked spaghetti. She cooked <u>spaghetti</u> with sauce.

   _____

   _____

Try It
Write five more sentences that use object pronouns.

1. _____

2. _____

3. _____

4. _____

5. _____

Lesson 1.7　Pronoun Agreement

A **pronoun** replaces a noun in a sentence. The noun that is replaced is called the **antecedent**. All pronouns have antecedents. Pronouns must agree in gender and number with their antecedents and what their antecedents refer to.

> Tony must bring his own lunch to the picnic.
> *He* must bring *his* own lunch to the picnic. (agrees in gender)
> Not: *He* must bring *her* own lunch to the picnic. (does not agree in gender)

> Tony must bring *three* lunches to the picnic.
> Tony must bring *them* to the picnic. (agrees in number)
> Not: Tony must bring *it* to the picnic. (does not agree in number)

Complete It

Circle the correct pronoun in parentheses. Remember that pronouns must agree in both gender and number.

1. Austin did well on (her, his) English report.

2. Austin didn't do well on (his, its) math test.

3. He missed eight problems. (He, They) were hard.

4. Charlotte did well on (her, his) math test.

5. Charlotte didn't do well on (her, them) English report.

6. She made six mistakes in grammar. (They, She) were spelling and punctuation errors.

7. Austin tutored Charlotte with (its, her) grammar skills.

8. Charlotte tutored Austin with (his, her) math skills.

9. Charlotte took Austin to dinner at (her, them) father's restaurant.

10. They ate a small veggie pizza. (Its, It) was delicious.

11. Charlotte and Austin also went to see a movie. (She, They) went to see a comedy.

12. The movie was funny, and (it, they) made them both laugh.

Lesson 1.7 Pronoun Agreement

Solve It
Solve the following riddle by choosing words from the box to fill in the blanks.

his	it
her	them

Who ate the pizza with pepper?

Who ate the pizza with _____?

Charlotte ate the pizza with pepper.

She ate _____ pizza with _____.

Who ordered a salad with tomatoes?

Who ordered a salad with _____?

Austin ordered the salad with tomatoes.

He ordered _____ salad with _____.

I like pizza with _____. (fill in your favorite)

I like pizza with _____. (word from the box)

I like salad with _____. (fill in your favorite)

I like salad with _____. (word from the box)

Try It
Write a letter to your best friend telling about a recent event at school. Include at least four pronouns and antecedents in your letter.

_____

_____

_____

_____

_____

_____

_____

_____

Lesson 1.8 Verbs: Regular Present and Past Tense

A **verb** is a word that tells the action or the state of being in a sentence.

> The dogs *sniff* the flowers.

In this sentence, *sniff* is the verb. It tells the action of the sentence. This sentence is in the present tense. The action is taking place now.

> Kevin *talked* about the game last night.

In this sentence, *talked* is the verb. It tells the action of the sentence. This sentence is in the past tense. The action took place in the past. Add **ed** to the present tense of a regular verb to make it past tense. If the word already ends in the letter **e**, just add the letter **d**.

Match It

Match the present tense verb forms in Column A with their past tense form in Column B.

Column A	Column B
add	whispered
ask	asked
call	yelled
dance	added
gasp	gasped
joke	warned
look	called
love	reported
note	danced
order	ordered
observe	noted
report	loved
warn	observed
whisper	looked
yell	joked

Lesson 1.8 Verbs: Regular Present and Past Tense

Complete It
Use the same words from page 20 to complete the following sentences. Choose the correct form, either present or past tense.

1. Quinten _____ a good question in science class earlier.

2. As they look at the picture, the ladies _____ at its beauty.

3. I _____ at the stars as I walk through the planetarium.

4. Kelly and Taylor, please _____ that in your report.

5. Shelly and Dylan _____ when they are late.

6. The spectators _____ and cheered many times during the game last night.

7. Jim fell on the ice. But he _____ about it later.

8. _____ the passengers, now!

9. May I have some milk? I want to _____ it to my coffee.

10. Carl _____ waffles for breakfast.

Try It
Write a fictional paragraph. Use at least three of the verbs from this lesson. Use their present or past tense forms, or both. Use at least three more verbs (present and/or past) of your own choosing.

_____

_____

_____

_____

_____

_____

_____

_____

_____

Lesson 1.9 Verbs: Irregular Present and Past Tense

Irregular verbs do not follow the same rules as regular verbs when forming their past tense. They must be learned. Below is a list of some of the common irregular verbs in their present and past tense forms.

Present:	Past:
am	was
begin	began
bring	brought
do	did
eat	ate
get	got
is	was
let	let
put	put
rise	rose
sleep	slept
think	thought

Rewrite It

Rewrite each sentence using a different tense. For example, if the sentence is in the present, rewrite it in the past. Remember, if you change the tense of the verb, forms of other words in the sentence may change also. Use a dictionary if you need help.

1. The teacher said to begin the test now.

_____

2. The cup broke when I dropped it.

_____

3. I drive my car to work.

_____

4. Michelle and Ray ate all of the pizza.

_____

5. I keep your secret.

_____

6. Let's make a cake for dessert.

_____

Lesson 1.9 Verbs: Irregular Present and Past Tense

Proof It

Proofread the following paragraph. Use the proofreading marks to delete the irregular present and past tense verbs that are used incorrectly. Write the correct word above the incorrect word. Use a dictionary if you need help.

_e_	- deletes words or letters
∧	- inserts words or letters

Do you knew the name of the very first national park? It was Yellowstone National Park. It is founded in 1872. Yellowstone sats in three states: Wyoming, Montana, and Idaho. Hot springs cut into the land of Yellowstone. Old Faithful and Mammoth Hot Springs got the most attention from visitors. The spray from Old Faithful can rose 150 feet into the air. Mammoth Hot Springs continues to grew to this day. Many animals lived in the park. Bears, mountain sheep, elk, bison, moose, and deer, and other wildlife made their home in Yellowstone National Park. Thousands of visitors came to the park every year.

Try It

Choose four present and four past tense irregular verbs from the list on page 22. Write a fictional paragraph using these verbs.

_____

_____

_____

_____

_____

_____

_____

Lesson 1.10 Action Verbs

Action verbs tell the action of the sentence. Action verbs come in both regular and irregular forms. They also have present, past, and future tense forms.

Sarah and Nancy *jump* rope at lunch time. (present)
Sarah and Nancy *jumped* rope after school yesterday. (past)
Sarah and Nancy *will jump* rope at lunch and after school tomorrow. (future)

Syd is going to *run* on the track team. (present)
Syd *ran* on the track team last year. (past)
Syd *will run* on the track team next year, too. (future)

Solve It
Complete the crossword puzzle using the words from the box.

bellowed	crashed	dug	throw
bounce	danced	skipped	travel

Across

3. Alan _____ for hours at the party.

4. The announcement _____ across the auditorium.

5. The students _____ for buried fossils.

6. Karen and Marc will _____ to the Caribbean for their vacations.

Down

1. The preschoolers _____ home from school.

2. The pan _____ to the floor when my sleeve caught the handle.

4. Which ball do you think will _____ the highest?

6. _____ the ball to me!

Lesson 1.10 Action Verbs

Identify It

Circle the action verb in each of the following sentences. Then, replace the verb with another action verb of your own.

1. The hungry travelers gulped the snacks.
2. Cami spun around and around in her new dress.
3. The papers fluttered around the room when the fan started.
4. The puppies yelped all night.
5. Kate and Brad sprung out of their seats.
6. Many birds crunched the seeds in the feeder.
7. The toddlers screamed with delight at the clown.
8. The corn kernels hopped in the hot oil.
9. The colorful photograph leapt off the page in the fashion magazine.
10. Bell's earrings sparkled in the sunlight.

Try It

Write a paragraph using ten action verbs that you did not use above.

_____

_____

_____

_____

_____

_____

_____

_____

_____

_____

_____

_____

_____

_____

Lesson 1.11   Helping Verbs

Helping verbs are not main verbs. Helping verbs help to form some of the tenses of main verbs. Helping verbs express time and mood.

Helping verbs:

shall	may
will	have
could	had
would	has
should	do
must	did
can	

She *could run* for miles and miles.

The forms of the verb *to be* are also helping verbs.

is   are   was   were   am   been

An **ing** verb is a clue that there is a helping verb in the sentence.

She *was running* for miles and miles.

Sometimes, more than one helping verb is used in a sentence. This is called a **verb phrase**.

She *had been running* for miles and miles.

Identify It

Circle the letter of the sentence that contains a helping verb. Remember, helping verbs help to set the time and mood of sentences.

1. a. We shall all go to the movies.
   b. We went to the movies.
   c. They ran to the movies.

2. a. Jake helped me with my homework.
   b. Jake will help me with my homework.
   c. Jake helps me with my homework every day.

3. a. I could study all night for the test.
   b. I studied for the test.
   c. I studied with Carol.

4. a. Cheryl only accepted the best.
   b. Cheryl accepted nothing less than perfection.
   c. Cheryl would accept nothing less.

5. a. I should think so!
   b. I think so.
   c. I think you are correct.

Lesson 1.11 Helping Verbs

Complete It

Choose a helping verb or verb phrase from the box to complete each sentence. Then, circle the main verb of the sentence. Sometimes there is a word between the helping and main verbs.

have	is	were
had	are	am
has	was	been

1. We _____ _____ planning our vacation for many months.

2. I _____ looking forward to it.

3. We _____ traveling by ship.

4. We _____ to visit a travel agent last week to get our tickets.

5. It _____ fun choosing the ship.

Try It

Write ten sentences using a different helping verb or verb phrase in each.

_____

_____

_____

_____

_____

_____

_____

_____

_____

_____

Lesson 1.12 Linking Verbs

Linking verbs are not main verbs. Linking verbs connect, or link, a subject to a noun or adjective. They do not express an action. A verb or adjective will follow these linking verbs in the sentence.

The most common linking verbs are the forms of the verb *be*:

What time *is* it?
We *are* ten minutes away.
What *was* that sound?
There *were* many people in line at the store.
I've *been* sick.
I *am* tired, Dad.

Other linking verbs are those of the five senses:

Do you *smell* that?
You don't *look* too good.
Did the milk *taste* funny?
I don't *feel* too well.
That plan *sounds* good.

Other linking verbs reflect a state of being:

You *appear* ready.
I *seem* better today.
You have *become* very tall.
Tom and Tammy *grow* happier every day.
I will *remain* here tonight.

Identify It

Circle the linking verb and underline the noun or adjective that is linked to the subject.

1. The book is good.

2. The flowers smell sweet.

3. The team appears disorganized.

4. The apples are bad.

5. Sharon looks fantastic tonight.

6. We were late.

7. The pear was tasty.

8. I am cold.

Lesson 1.12 Linking Verbs

Rewrite It

Rewrite each of the sentences with a linking verb from the box. Notice how using other forms of linking verbs add variety to your sentences.

grows	been	sounds
has	remained	tastes

1. The water from the faucet is bad.

   _____

2. The older woman in the play is weary.

   _____

3. The trip is long.

   _____

4. Walking, instead of riding, is great.

   _____

5. The team is disorganized after half time.

   _____

Try It

Write a paragraph using at least eight of the linking verbs on page 28. Remember, linking verbs link the subject of the sentence to either a noun or an adjective.

_____

_____

_____

_____

_____

_____

_____

_____

_____

Lesson 1.13 Subject-Verb Agreement

Verbs must agree in number with the subject of the sentence. If the subject is singular, use a singular verb. If the subject is plural, make sure to use a plural verb.

The shirt *fits* just right.   The movies *were* sold out.

If the subject is a **compound subject**, two or more subjects, connected by the word *and*, then a plural verb is needed.

Erika and Chris *photograph* the birds.   Erika *photographs* the birds.

If the subject is a compound subject connected by the words *or* or *nor*, then the verb will agree with the subject that is closer to the verb.

Neither Wanita nor Susan *likes* chocolate pie. (Susan likes)
Does Wanita or her sisters *like* chocolate pie? (sisters like)

If the subject and the verb are separated by a word or words, be sure that the verb still agrees with the subject.

Susan, as well as her coworkers, *wants* to complete the project. (Susan wants)

If the subject is a **collective noun**, a singular word that represents a group, like *family* and *team*, then a singular verb is generally used.

The family *is* ready to go.   The team *runs* one mile every day.

When using the phrases *there is, there are, here is,* and *here are,* make sure that the subjects and verbs agree.

There is one piece of pizza left.   Here is the right path to take.
There are many pieces left.   Here are the bikes we're supposed to use.

Complete It
Circle the correct verb for each sentence.

1. Troy (help, helps) his sister with her homework after school.

2. Troy and Billy (help, helps) their sister with her homework after school.

3. Does Sally or her brothers (bike, bikes) to school?

4. There (is, are) one store that I like at that mall.

5. Here (is, are) the books on that subject.

Lesson 1.13 Subject-Verb Agreement

Proof It
Proofread the following paragraph, correcting the subject-verb agreement mistakes as you go. Use the proofreading key to mark the mistakes and insert the correction.

- deletes words or letters
∧ - inserts words or letters

Tiger Woods' real first name is Eldrick, and he were born on December 30, 1975. Fans all over the world salutes him as one of the greatest golfers of all time. He became a professional golfer in 1996. In 2001, Tiger held all four professional major championships at one time, the first golfer ever to do so. He were also the first golfer of African American or Asian descent to win a major championship. No sportsperson have ever been awarded <u>Sports Illustrated</u> Sportsman of the Year twice—except Tiger. Tiger and his father started the Tiger Woods Foundation. The foundation support community-based programs that promote health, education, and welfare for children. So, how did Tiger gets his nickname? Tiger were named after a Vietnamese soldier who was a friend of his father. Tiger's father had given the same nickname to his friend.

Try It
Write a paragraph with four sentences about your favorite sport. Be sure that the subjects and verbs agree.

_____

_____

_____

_____

_____

_____

_____

_____

Lesson 1.14 Adjectives

Adjectives are words used to describe a noun or pronoun. Using colorful, lively, descriptive adjectives makes writing and speaking more interesting.

Most adjectives are **common adjectives** and are not capitalized. They can be found before or after the noun they describe.

It was a *breezy* day.   The day was *breezy*.

The adjective *breezy* tells something about, or describes, the noun *day*.

Proper adjectives are formed from proper nouns and are always capitalized.

The chef likes baking his pizzas in the *Italian* oven.

The proper adjective *Italian* describes what kind of oven it is.

Solve It
Unscramble the words to reveal adjectives that might describe a butterfly.

1. e b f a u t u l i _____

2. r o f c l o l u _____

3. t e r p t y _____

4. g r h i t b _____

Now write a list of ten adjectives that describe your favorite animals.

Animal: _____

1. _____   6. _____

2. _____   7. _____

3. _____   8. _____

4. _____   9. _____

5. _____   10. _____

Lesson 1.14 Adjectives

Rewrite It

Add an adjective that describes each noun in bold. Remember, adjectives can come before or after the noun they describe.

Candice and Danny were 12-year-old twins. They

wanted a _____ **pet** for their birthday.

"Do you want a **dog** that is _____ or a **cat** that is

_____?" asked their mother.

"You must understand," their mother continued, "pets are a _____

responsibility. Are you ready for this responsibility?"

Candice and Danny were ready. They were always kind to animals, and they

were ready for this _____ **job**.

On their birthday, Candice and Danny's _____ **parents** took them

to their local animal shelter. There, they found a **dog** that was _____ and

a _____ **cat**.

Try It

Write a paragraph about your favorite movie using ten different adjectives.

_____

_____

_____

_____

_____

_____

_____

_____

_____

_____

_____

Lesson 1.15 Adverbs

Adverbs are words used to describe a verb, an adjective, or another adverb. An adverb tells *how*, *why*, *when*, *where*, *how often*, and *how much*. Adverbs often end in **ly** (but not always).

                How?   **Where?**
John drove *carefully* on the slick road. The weather *outside* was rainy. It seemed

    How often?   **When?**   **How?**
like it would *never* stop raining. *Tomorrow*, *hopefully* the weather will be better.

Identify It
Circle the letter of the sentence that contains an adverb. Remember, adverbs modify verbs, adjectives, and other adverbs.

1. a. Lisa quickly finished work so she could go to dinner.
   b. Lisa finished work so she could go to dinner.
   c. Lisa did not finish her work.

2. a. Rachel cooked as if for a feast.
   b. Rachel didn't cook.
   c. Rachel cooked the meal today so it would be ready for the feast.

3. a. Fruit makes a delicious dessert.
   b. Fruit often makes a delicious dessert.
   c. Fruit is dessert.

4. a. The kittens purr very loudly when they are sleeping.
   b. The kittens purr.
   c. The kittens purr when they sleep.

5. a. Birds eat seeds.
   b. Birds eat tiny seeds from a feeder.
   c. Birds eat many tiny seeds from the feeder in the winter.

6. a. The snow falling outside is beautiful.
   b. The snow is beautiful.
   c. The snowballs are cold and sticky.

7. a. Please ask the clerk if they have more berries.
   b. Please politely ask the clerk if they have more berries.
   c. Please ask the clerk if they have more fresh berries.

Lesson 1.15 Adverbs

Identify It

Circle the adverbs in the following paragraphs. Then, underline the verb, adjective, or other adverb they describe.

The Emperor's New Clothes, The Snow Queen, and The Little Mermaid are just a few fairy tales written by a remarkably famous writer. Who so colorfully wrote about a little match girl, a brave tin soldier, and an ugly duckling? Hans Christian Andersen did.

Hans Christian Andersen was born poor in 1805 in a town in Denmark. What extra money the family had they eagerly spent at the theatre. When they didn't have money for tickets, Hans would quietly sit outside the theatre actively reading the playbill. He knew he would definitely follow his love of literature and the theatre as a career. With help from grant money, Hans completed school at the University of Copenhagen and became a writer. He wrote more than 150 fairy tales. They have been translated into more than 100 languages. The Ugly Duckling, a tale of self-discovery, was considered by some experts to be an autobiography. Hans also wrote plays, poetry, and travelogues. Hans Christian Andersen remains one of the world's best known and most translated authors.

Try It

Write ten sentences with at least one adverb in each.

1. _____
2. _____
3. _____
4. _____
5. _____
6. _____
7. _____
8. _____
9. _____
10. _____

Lesson 1.16 Conjunctions

Conjunctions are connectors. They connect individual words or groups of words in sentences. There are three kinds of conjunctions.

Coordinate conjunctions connect words, phrases, or clauses, using words like *and*, *but*, and *or*.

> The snow is cold *and* fluffy.
> Chris likes soccer, *but* Samantha likes football.

Correlative conjunctions are used with pairs and are used together. *Both/and*, *either/or*, and *neither/nor* are examples of correlative conjunctions.

> *Both* Tammy *and* Tara went to the play. (*Tammy* and *Tara* are a pair.)

Subordinate conjunctions connect two clauses that are not equal. They connect dependent clauses to independent clauses. *After*, *as long as, since*, and *while* are examples of subordinate conjunctions.

> They run *after* the sun goes down. (dependent clause: *after the sun goes down*)

Complete It
Complete the following sentences with a conjunction from the box.

and	both/and	neither/nor	as long as
but	either/or	after	since

1. Tabitha wanted to have pretzels for a snack _____ Kisha wanted snowcones.

2. _____ red _____ orange was used in the mural.

3. Taylor wanted to go skiing today _____ the big snowfall.

4. Kari didn't go biking _____ it was storming.

5. _____ Buster _____ Buzz passed puppy training class.

6. Trevor wanted to stay inside and play board games _____

    it was still raining.

7. _____ take out the trash _____ walk the dog.

8. We were going to see a movie, _____ we went out to eat, instead.

Lesson 1.16 Conjunctions

Identify It

Identify the conjunctions in the following sentences as coordinate, correlative, or subordinate. Write **CD** for coordinate, **CR** for correlative, or **S** for subordinate after each sentence.

1. _____ Are we going to go biking or hiking on Saturday?

2. _____ Neither pasta nor pizza was offered on the menu.

3. _____ As long as it's raining, we may as well get our homework done.

4. _____ Either Rachel or Carrie will be voted president of the class.

5. _____ Let's walk to school since it is a sunny, warm day.

6. _____ Todd wants to play baseball this weekend but he has a class in the morning.

7. _____ While we are waiting in line, let's get some popcorn.

8. _____ Both the girls and the boys' teams are going to the championship.

9. _____ Grant wants mushrooms and peppers on his pizza.

10. _____ After this week, there's only six weeks of school this year.

Try It

Write five sentences of your own using the conjunctions. Use two conjunctions from each category.

1. _____

_____

2. _____

_____

3. _____

_____

4. _____

_____

5. _____

_____

Lesson 1.17 Interjections

An **interjection** is a one- or two-word phrase used to express surprise or strong emotion.

<u>Common interjections:</u>

Ah	Hurray
Aha	Oh
Alas	Ouch
Aw	Uh
Cheers	Uh-huh
Eh	Uh-uh
Hey	Well
Hi	Wow
Huh	Yeah

An exclamation mark is usually used after an interjection to separate it from the rest of the sentence.

Oh! I'm so happy that you can make the trip!

If the feeling isn't quite as strong, a comma is used in place of the exclamation point.

Oh, that's too bad he won't be joining us.

Sometimes question marks are used as an interjection's punctuation.

Eh? Is that really true?

Find It

Use a dictionary to look up each of the following interjections. Write the word's part of speech and the dictionary definition. Then, use each interjection in a sentence.

1. ah - _____

_____

2. alas - _____

_____

3. eh - _____

_____

4. hey - _____

_____

5. oh - _____

_____

6. ouch - _____

_____

Lesson 1.17 Interjections

Rewrite It

Carl and Dylan are trying to get a game of backyard baseball started. Rewrite the dialogue to include interjections that will make the passage more lively and fun to read.

"Dylan, are you coming?" Carl yelled up to Dylan's open window. He saw Dylan grab his bat. "Everyone's waiting! And don't forget your mitt!"

"What did you say? I can't hear you." Dylan shouted from somewhere in the house. A second later, he opened the front door and jumped off the front porch, skipping the three steps. He did not have his mitt.

"I told you not to forget your mitt!" Carl rolled his eyes. Dylan was always forgetting something.

"I've got it right here," Dylan pulled his mitt out from behind him with a big grin. "I heard you the whole time!"

"You're funny! Now, let's get going! We'll be lucky if we get there by the seventh-inning stretch!"

_____

_____

_____

_____

_____

_____

_____

_____

_____

_____

_____

_____

_____

_____

_____

Lesson 1.18 Prepositions

Prepositions are words or groups of words that show the relationship between a noun or pronoun (the object of the sentence) and another word in the sentence. A prepositional phrase includes the preposition, the object of the preposition, and the modifiers (describes other words) of the object. Prepositional phrases tell about *when* or *where* something is happening.

> The students walked **across** the street.
> (*across* is the preposition; *street* is the object; *across the street* is the prepositional phrase)

> The students walked **alongside** the small park.
> (*alongside* is the preposition; *park* is the object; *small* is the modifier; *alongside the small park* is the prepositional phrase)

Common prepositions:

above	behind	for	over
across	below	from	to
after	beneath	in	toward
along	beside	inside	under
around	between	into	until
at	by	near	up
away	down	off	with
because	during	on	within
before	except	outside	without

Identify It

Identify the preposition, object, and modifier in each of the following sentences. Write a **P** above the preposition, an **O** above the object, and an **M** above the modifier.

1. The students played outside at the late recess.

2. The horse jumped over the high fence.

3. Alice walked out of the scary movie.

4. Timmy looked down the deep well.

5. The paper fell underneath the small bookcase.

Lesson 1.18 Prepositions

Solve It
Write a preposition that answers the questions below. Use the list of page 40 if you need help.

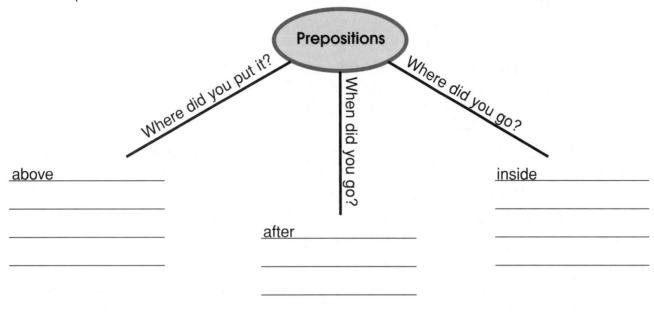

above _____

_____

_____

after _____

_____

_____

_____

inside _____

_____

_____

Try It
Write a journal entry about what you did yesterday. Use at least six prepositions. Once you have written your entry, underline all of the prepositions you used.

_____
_____
_____
_____
_____
_____
_____
_____
_____
_____
_____
_____
_____

Lesson 1.19 Articles

Articles are specific words that serve as adjectives before a noun. *A, an,* and *the* are articles.

The is a **definite article**. It names a specific noun.
> I want to go to *the* park where everyone else went.
> (The article *the* shows that the person wants to go to a specific park.)

A and *an* are **indefinite articles**. They do not name a specific noun.
> I would like to go to *a* park this weekend.
> (The article *a* shows that the person wants to go to any park, and it doesn't matter which one.)

Use *a* when the noun it precedes begins with a consonant or a vowel that sounds like a consonant.
> a dress   a certificate   a book bag   a one-way street

Use *an* when the noun it precedes begins with a vowel or vowel sound.
> an eyebrow   an ostrich   an apple   an honest person

Match It
Match the object in each set with the article that goes with it. Draw a line from Column A to the correct article in Column B. Then, in Column C, write the article and noun together.

Column A	Column B	Column C
nonspecific play	a	_____
specific play	an	_____
nonspecific envelope	the	_____

Column A	Column B	Column C
specific beach	a	_____
nonspecific beach	an	_____
nonspecific art piece	the	_____

Column A	Column B	Column C
nonspecific hero	a	_____
nonspecific umbrella	an	_____
specific umbrella	the	_____

Lesson 1.19 Articles

Proof It

Proofread the following paragraph. Look for mistakes in the use of articles. Use the proof marks to delete incorrect words and insert the correct words.

e - deletes words or letters
∧ - inserts words or letters

You've probably read much about the White House, a Washington Memorial, and an Lincoln Memorial in Washington, D.C. But how much do you know about a U.S. Capitol Building? The U.S. Capitol is not just an building in Washington, D.C. It is symbolically and architecturally important. It also has practical significance. The U.S. Capitol is the home of a House of Representatives and the Senate. If visiting Washington, D.C., an dome at the east end of an National Mall on Capitol Hill gives the U.S. Capitol away. The U.S. Capitol is also considered to be the museum. Inside, a eager visitor can find many examples of American art and history. The U.S. Capitol is an symbol of a American government.

Try It

Write a paragraph with five sentences about a local landmark. Once you have finished your paragraph, underline the articles.

_____

_____

_____

_____

_____

_____

_____

_____

_____

Review Chapter I Lessons I-19

Review: Common Nouns, Proper Nouns, Regular Plurals, Irregular Plurals, Subject Pronouns, Object Pronouns, Pronoun Agreement

Putting It Together
Answer the following questions by circling the letter of the best answer.

1. Which sentence contains a common noun?
   a. I visited Yellowstone National Park.
   b. I liked seeing the animals.
   c. I heard that you went to Everglades National Park.

2. Which sentence contains a proper noun?
   a. The U.S. Capitol is in Washington D.C.
   b. History is one of my favorite subjects.
   c. I like to study science.

3. Which sentence contains a regular plural noun?
   a. I liked seeing the moose at the park.
   b. The geese were in the pond and then they flew overhead.
   c. The cats liked playing together.

4. Which sentence contains an irregular plural noun?
   a. The dogs loved playing in the water.
   b. Rabbits make great pets.
   c. The mice scurried under the floorboards.

5. Which sentence contains a subject pronoun?
   a. Ava went on a science field tip.
   b. She went on a science field trip.
   c. Aaron went on a science field trip.

6. Which sentence contains an object pronoun?
   a. The team captain picked me.
   b. The team captain picked Sandy to play.
   c. He picked the best player to be on his side.

7. Which sentence has an incorrect use of pronoun agreement?
   a. The brothers left his jackets on the field.
   b. Diane picked up her books at the library.
   c. Jason forgot his books at the library.

Review Chapter 1 Lessons 1–19

Review: Regular Past Tense Verbs, Irregular Past Tense Verbs, Action Verbs, Helping Verbs, Linking Verbs, Verb Agreement

Draw a line from the word or phrase in Column A with the word or phrase that it describes in Column B.

Column A	Column B
1. sound	Past Tense Regular Verb
2. The books are heavy.	Past Tense Irregular Verb
3. should	Action Verb
4. taught	Helping Verb
5. whispered	Linking Verb
6. throw	Subject/Verb Agreement

Review: Adjectives, Adverbs, Conjunctions, Interjections, Prepositions, Articles

Write the part of speech above the words in bold. Write **ADJ** for adjectives, **ADV** for adverbs, **CONJ** for conjunctions, **INT** for interjections, **PREP** for prepositions, and **ART** for articles.

Hurray! Happy Birthday!

Birthdays were **first** celebrated **in ancient** Rome. **The** Romans celebrated **the** birthdays **of** their **favorite** gods **and important** people, like **the** emperor. **In** Britain, they celebrate **the Queen's** birthday. **In the** United States, **the** birthdays **of** presidents **and important** leaders, like Martin Luther King, are celebrated. **In** Japan, Korea, **and** China, the **sixtieth** birthday marks **a** transition **from an active** life **to** one **of** contemplation. **Many Eastern** cultures don't even recognize **the actual** date **of** birth. When **the first** moon **of the new** year arrives, everyone is **one year** older.

Lesson 1.20 Declarative Sentences

Declarative sentences are sentences that make statements. They say something about a place, person, thing, or idea. When punctuating a declarative sentence, use a period at the end of the sentence.

> Henry Bergh was the founder of the American Society for the Prevention of Cruelty to Animals.
> Pizza is my favorite food.
> Marathons are 26.2 miles long.

Identify It

Place a check mark in front of each declarative sentence. Leave the other sentences blank.

1. _____ Venice is a city in Italy.

2. _____ Venice has a network of canals used for transportation.

3. _____ Have you ever been to Venice?

4. _____ The Grand Canal is the main thoroughfare.

5. _____ Three bridges cross the Grand Canal.

6. _____ How many bridges cross the Grand Canal?

7. _____ Look at the beautiful bridge!

8. _____ Venice has a very temperate climate.

9. _____ How warm does it get in Venice in the summer?

10. _____ Venice is one of the most beautiful cities in Europe.

Lesson 1.20 Declarative Sentences

Proof It

Make sure that each declarative sentence ends in a period. If the punctuation is correct, place a check mark before the sentence. If not, use the proofreading marks to make each declarative sentence end with a period.

> ⊙ – inserts periods
> ℓ – deletes punctuation

1. _____ I want to play baseball tomorrow.

2. _____ I can't wait to go to the gym with Greg and Sarah?

3. _____ If you order pizza, make sure to get onions.

4. _____ Do you see the rainbow?

5. _____ Jen said that it is time to eat?

Try It

Write a dialogue between two people. Write ten sentences about a place they are visiting. Be sure to use periods when you are making declarative sentences.

_____

_____

_____

_____

_____

_____

_____

_____

_____

_____

_____

_____

_____

_____

_____

_____

_____

Lesson 1.21 Interrogative Sentences

Interrogative sentences are sentences that ask questions. When punctuating an interrogative sentence, use a question mark.

> Did I see lightning in the sky**?**
> Do you like fresh spinach in your salad**?**
> Do you run in the morning or in the evening**?**

Complete It

Complete the following sentences by circling the correct punctuation.

1. Alla walked briskly five times around the block (. ?)
2. Did you see the famous statue on your vacation (. ?)
3. The spider spun a beautiful web (. ?)
4. Did the poem inspire your artwork (. ?)
5. How quickly did you complete the obstacle course (. ?)
6. The designer showed great style (. ?)
7. I like the rhythm of that song (. ?)
8. Did your dad make spaghetti for dinner last night (. ?)
9. Are you going to try out for the wrestling team (. ?)
10. Do you lift weights to strengthen your muscles (. ?)
11. Are those chestnuts I smell roasting (. ?)
12. My friends are coming over after dinner (. ?)
13. I think the batteries are dead in that radio (. ?)
14. Aren't the pictures in the museum beautiful (. ?)
15. Where are you going after school (. ?)
16. Who is at the door (. ?)
17. Jon and I walked around the block (. ?)
18. The baseball game starts at seven o'clock tonight (. ?)
19. What time did you say (. ?)
20. Arlene and Beth joined a book club (. ?)

Lesson 1.21 Interrogative Sentences

Solve It

A farmer is taking a student on a tour of his garden. The student has many questions about what kind of vegetables he grows. The farmer's answers are given, but the student's questions are missing. Write the question with the appropriate punctuation in the space provided. The first one has been done for you.

1. How many vegetables do you grow?   I grow many vegetables.

2. _____   I grow mostly soy beans.

3. _____   My favorite vegetable is broccoli.

4. _____   If you want to be a farmer, you should study many subjects, but especially science, math, and social studies.

Try It

Write a list of questions you might ask a local business owner.

_____

_____

_____

_____

_____

_____

_____

_____

_____

_____

_____

Lesson 1.22 Exclamatory Sentences

Exclamatory sentences are sentences that reveal urgency, strong surprise, or emotion. When punctuating an exclamatory sentence, use an exclamation mark.

> I can't believe you ate the whole pie!
> Look at how much weight he is lifting!
> I think I smell a skunk!

Only use exclamation points when expressing urgency and strong surprise or emotion. Exclamation marks can also be used in dialogue, when the character or speaker is making an urgent or emotional statement.

Identify It

Identify which sentences are exclamatory by putting an exclamation mark at the end of the sentences. If it's not exclamatory, leave it blank.

1. Watch out for the ice

2. Ouch! I can't believe I stubbed my toe on the table again

3. Where are you having dinner tonight

4. The storm is quickly coming our way

5. I'm not sure if I want to go to the movies or not

6. It is so cold I think I have frostbite

7. Don't you like the cold weather

8. Ah! The sunset is gorgeous

9. You're it

10. Oh no! The bridge is out

11. What time is it

12. Oranges are my favorite fruit

13. Watch out! The oranges fell off the display

14. The Lord of the Rings is my favorite series of books

15. That author really inspires me

Lesson 1.22 Exclamatory Sentences

Rewrite It

Read the following postcard from one friend to another. The writer seems excited about her trip, but doesn't express it in her writing. Rewrite the postcard changing declarative sentences to exclamatory ones.

Dear Linda,

I'm having a wonderful time in Florida. The weather is fantastic. It's been sunny every day. We went swimming in the hotel's pool on Tuesday. Then, on Wednesday, we actually swam in the ocean. Tomorrow we are going to visit a marine animal sanctuary. Do you remember studying about the rescued marine animals in school? I can't wait to see the fish and animals. I wish you were here. See you soon.

Drew

_____

_____

_____

_____

_____

_____

Try It

Write a postcard to a friend or relative about a trip you have taken recently. Make it exciting by including exclamatory sentences. Make sentences exclamatory when you really want them to stand out.

_____

_____

_____

_____

_____

Lesson 1.23 Imperative Sentences

Imperative sentences demand that an action be performed. The subjects of imperative sentences are usually not expressed. They usually contain the understood subject *you*. Imperative sentences can be punctuated with a period or an exclamation mark. Use an exclamation mark in the same instances as you would for an exclamatory sentence, such as expressing urgency, surprise, or strong emotion.

Look at the rabbit behind the trees.
(*You* look at the rabbit behind the trees.)

Write the note here.
(*You* write the note here.)

Throw me the ball!
(*You* throw me the ball!)

Complete It
Choose a verb from the box that will complete each imperative sentence and write it on the line provided. Remember, the subject *you* is implied in the sentences.

carry	drive	pick	swing	vote
drink	pass	shoot	throw	yell

1. _____ for Simon for president!

2. _____ the potatoes, please.

3. _____ up the paper from the floor.

4. _____ that bag for your aunt.

5. _____ the ball to second base!

6. _____ slowly when on ice.

7. _____ the racket higher.

8. _____ the cheers louder!

9. _____ all of your tomato juice.

10. _____ the basketball through the hoop!

Lesson 1.23 Imperative Sentences

Find It

Use a thesaurus to find other imperative words that are synonyms of the imperative words below.

1. call - _____
2. carry – _____
3. drink – _____
4. drive – _____
5. look – _____
6. pass – _____
7. pick – _____
8. run – _____
9. shoot – _____
10. stop – _____

Try It

Write ten imperative sentences using the synonyms from the activity above. Remember to use correct punctuation.

1. _____
2. _____
3. _____
4. _____
5. _____
6. _____
7. _____
8. _____
9. _____
10. _____

Lesson 1.24 Simple Sentences

Simple sentences are sentences with one independent clause. **Independent clauses** present a complete thought and can stand alone as a sentence. Simple sentences do not have any dependent clauses. **Dependent clauses** do not present a complete thought and cannot stand alone as sentences.

Simple sentences can have one or more subjects.
> The *costumes* glittered.
> The *costumes* and the *jewelry* glittered.

Simple sentences can have one or more **predicates**, or verbs.
> The costumes *glittered*.
> The costumes *glittered* and *sparkled*.

Simple sentences can have more than one subject and more than one predicate.
> The *costumes* and the *jewelry glittered* and *sparkled*.

Identify It
Underline the subject or subjects in the following simple sentences.

1. Elsa, Tanya's mom, liked baking cookies.

2. Elsa liked baking cookies and cooking spaghetti.

3. Elsa and Tanya liked baking and cooking together.

4. Elsa liked baking and cooking.

5. Elsa liked baking better.

6. Tanya liked baking and cooking.

7. Tanya liked cooking better.

8. Tanya liked eating her mom's cookies.

9. Elsa liked eating her daughter's spaghetti.

10. Tanya's friends liked coming to dinner.

Lesson 1.24 Simple Sentences

Identify It
Underline the predicate or predicates in the following simple sentences.

1. Elsa, Tanya's mom, liked baking cookies.

2. Elsa liked baking cookies and cooking spaghetti.

3. Elsa and Tanya liked baking and cooking together.

4. Elsa liked baking and cooking.

5. Elsa liked baking better.

6. Tanya liked baking and cooking.

7. Tanya liked cooking better.

8. Tanya liked eating her mom's cookies.

9. Elsa liked eating her daughter's spaghetti.

10. Tanya's friends liked eating cookies and spaghetti.

Try It
Write ten simple sentences of your own. Remember, simple sentences may have more than one subject and more than one predicate.

_____

_____

_____

_____

_____

_____

_____

_____

_____

_____

_____

Lesson 1.25 Compound Sentences

Compound sentences are sentences with two or more simple sentences (independent clauses) joined by a coordinate conjunction, punctuation, or both. As in simple sentences, there are no dependent clauses in compound sentences.

A compound sentence can be joined by a comma and a coordinate conjunction.
 The costumes glittered, *but* the jewelry was dull.

A compound sentence can also be two simple sentences joined by a semicolon.
 The costumes glittered; the jewelry was dull.

Match It

Match simple sentences in Column A with simple sentences in Column B to create compound sentences. Add either a comma with a coordinate conjunction or a semicolon.

Column A	**Column B**
1. The seats were bad.	The snack bar line was long.
2. The actors were funny.	We can stay late.
3. The intermission was short.	The show was good.
4. The ushers were nice.	The ticket takers were rude.
5. We can leave early.	The orchestra played well.
6. The theater lights were low.	The actors were serious.
7. The audience laughed.	The audience applauded.
8. The actors' voices were loud.	The seats were sold out.
9. The play had good reviews.	The music was soft.
10. The actors bowed.	The stage lights were bright.

Lesson 1.25 Compound Sentences

Solve It

Combine each pair of simple sentences into a compound sentence.

Simple Sentences

1. Richard likes apples. Jackie likes pears.

2. Jackie likes skating. Richard likes running.

3. Richard likes dancing. Jackie likes singing.

4. Jackie likes summer. Richard likes winter.

5. Richard likes math. Jackie likes science.

Compound Sentences

1. _____

2. _____

3. _____

4. _____

5. _____

Try It

Continue to write about what Richard and Jackie each like and don't like. Write three more sentences for each character. Then, combine the sentences to form compound sentences.

Richard

_____

_____

_____

Jackie

_____

_____

_____

Compound Sentences

_____

_____

_____

Lesson 1.26 Complex Sentences

Complex sentences have one independent clause and two or more dependent clauses. The independent and dependent clauses are connected with a subordinate conjunction or a relative pronoun. Remember, dependent clauses do not present a complete thought and cannot stand alone as sentences. The dependent clause can be anywhere in the sentence.

Common subordinate conjunctions include *after, although, as, because, before, if, since, when, where, while, until,* and *unless.*

One complex sentence (connected with subordinate conjunction):
> *Since* he got a math tutor, his math grades have improved.

The independent and dependent clauses can also be connected with relative pronouns like *who, whose, which,* and *that.*

One complex sentence (connected with relative pronoun):
> Mr. Addy, *who* is a math teacher, tutors Ashton.

Combining simple sentences into complex sentences adds variety and clarity to writing.

Identify It
Circle the letter that best answers each question.

1. Which of the following sentences contains two simple, individual sentences?
   a. He is wearing his baseball uniform. He is holding his baseball bat.
   b. He is wearing his baseball uniform and holding his baseball bat.
   c. He is wearing his baseball uniform, although the game was cancelled.

2. Which of the following sentences contains a compound sentence?
   a. She is eating a salad. She is drinking lemonade.
   b. She is eating a salad, and she is drinking lemonade.
   c. She is drinking lemonade, since she is thirsty.

3. Which of the following sentences contains a complex sentence?
   a. Mary went jogging. Rose went jogging.
   b. Mary and Rose went jogging.
   c. Before breakfast, Mary and Rose went jogging.

4. Which of the following sentences contains a complex sentence?
   a. Mike was learning about moose at school. Mike was learning about caribou at school.
   b. Mike and Gil were learning about arctic animals at school.
   c. Mike, who loved animals, was learning about moose and caribou at school.

Lesson 1.26 Complex Sentences

Rewrite It
Rewrite the following article combining simple sentences to make compound and complex sentences.

Why would a ten-week old piglet wander the streets of New York City? New York City animal control officers asked the same question. One Friday afternoon they found a tiny piglet. They thought she had escaped from a market. They took her to a shelter. She was treated for wounds on her legs. She was treated for a respiratory infection. The shelter staff named her Priscilla. A local sanctuary took her in. They treated her. She was quite sick. Now she is healthy. Priscilla was adopted by a family in Michigan. She loves her new home.

_____

_____

_____

_____

_____

_____

_____

_____

_____

_____

Try It
Write an article about an event in your school using compound and complex sentences. Include at least three complex and two compound sentences in your article.

_____

_____

_____

_____

_____

_____

_____

Lesson 1.27 Sentence Fragments

A **sentence fragment** is a group of words that is missing either a subject or a verb. A sentence fragment is also a group of words that doesn't express a complete thought, as in a dependent clause.

Takes a walk every day at lunch. (no subject)
Complete Sentence: *Sandy* takes a walk every day at lunch.

A walk every day at lunch. (no subject and no verb)
Complete Sentence: *Sandy takes* a walk every day at lunch.

Since the line was so long. (not a complete thought)
Complete Sentence: *We went to a different restaurant*, since the line was
so long.

Match It
The sentences in Column A are sentence fragments. Choose a group of words from Column B that will complete the sentence and make it whole. Write the new sentences on the line.

Column A	Column B
1. is the twelfth month of the year.	December has two birthstones,
2. Until 46 B.C.,	December
3. Several European countries	Orville Wright made the first heavier-than-air flight at Kitty Hawk, North Carolina
4. turquoise and zircon.	celebrate December 6th as the Feast of Saint Nicholas.
5. on December 17, 1903.	December had only 29 days.

_____
_____
_____
_____
_____
_____
_____
_____

Lesson 1.27 Sentence Fragments

Identify It

Now that you have completed the 5 sentences, identify why the sentences in Column A are fragments. Write *missing a subject*, *missing a verb*, or *missing a subject and a verb*.

1. _____
2. _____
3. _____
4. _____
5. _____

Try It

When is your birthday? Write ten complete sentences about the month of your birth. Make sure all of your sentences are complete, with a subject, a verb, and express complete thoughts. Once you have completed your sentences, circle the subjects and underline the verbs.

1. _____
2. _____
3. _____
4. _____
5. _____
6. _____
7. _____
8. _____
9. _____
10. _____

Lesson 1.28 Combining Sentences

Combining short, choppy sentences into longer more detailed sentences makes writing much more interesting and much easier to read. Sentences can be combined in a variety of ways.

Compound subjects and compound verbs:

> Brad went on a hiking trip. C.J. went on a hiking trip.
> *Brad and C.J.* went on a hiking trip.
>
> We hiked on our long weekend away. We biked on our long weekend away.
> We *hiked and biked* on our long weekend away.

Adjectives and adverbs:

> I ate an orange for breakfast. The orange was sweet.
> I ate a *sweet orange* for breakfast.
>
> Abby walked through the foggy forest. Abby walked slowly.
> Abby *walked slowly* through the foggy forest.

Making complex sentences (using subordinate conjunctions):

> The class was going on a camping trip. They were going on the trip providing it didn't rain.
> The class was going on a camping trip *providing it didn't rain.*

Rewrite It
Rewrite these simple sentences into compound or complex sentences.

1. Rachel went to the carnival on Saturday. Dan went to the carnival on Saturday.

   _____

2. The popcorn crackled as it popped. The popcorn snapped as it popped.

   _____

3. Nancy investigated the old trunk. Nancy investigated the brown trunk.

   _____

4. Carson excitedly spoke about his journey. Carson loudly spoke about his journey.

   _____

5. We can stop for breakfast. We can stop for breakfast if it is quick.

   _____

Lesson 1.28 Combining Sentences

Identify It

Draw a line to match the sentences on the left with the type of combined sentences they are on the right.

1. So that the birthday party remains a surprise, we must get there on time.

   compound subjects

2. Helen and Tammy brought sweaters as presents.

   combining adjectives

3. Helen brought a purple, knit sweater.

   complex sentence

---

4. Ginger liked raspberry, lemon cake.

   compound verbs

5. Because it was her birthday, Ginger's mom baked her favorite cake.

   combining adjectives

6. Ginger's mother cooked and baked for hours.

   complex sentence

---

7. Ginger and her friends had a great time at the party.

   compound subjects

8. Ginger greatly appreciated the presents.

   combining adverbs

9. Although it was late, the friends stayed for more cake.

   complex sentence

Try It

Pretend that you are a reporter covering a birthday party. Write an account of the party. Use adjective and adverbs and both compound and complex sentences.

_____

_____

_____

_____

_____

_____

_____

_____

_____

Lesson 1.29 Writing a Paragraph

A **paragraph** is made up of a group of sentences. A paragraph should have, and stick to, a single topic. Each sentence should focus on the topic with plenty of information and supporting details related to the topic.

Elements of a Paragraph: There are three parts to a paragraph.

1. Beginning: The topic sentence is the beginning of the paragraph. It tells the reader what the paragraph is going to be about. It also expresses the feeling of the paragraph.

2. Middle: The middle is the main part of the paragraph. The sentences here give more information and supporting details about the topic sentence.

3. End: After all of the information and details are written, the ending sentence concludes, or sums up, the paragraph's main idea.

Writing the Paragraph: There are five steps for writing a paragraph.

1. Prewriting: Choose your topic and think about what information and details you want to include.

2. Drafting: Write your topic sentence and the other parts of your paragraph.

3. Revising: Reread your paragraph. Make sure the three parts of your paragraph are used correctly. Rewrite your paragraph and include details with adjectives and adverbs to make it more interesting.

4. Proofreading: Proofread your paragraph looking for errors in spelling and punctuation.

5. Publishing: Now's your chance to show off your work. You will publish your paragraph.

Types of Paragraphs: A few of the most common paragraphs include the following:

Descriptive: Descriptive paragraphs give vivid details of people, places, things, or ideas.

Narrative: Narrative paragraphs give the details of an event or events in the form of a story.

Expository: Expository paragraphs give facts or explain ideas in a nonfiction format.

Persuasive: Persuasive paragraphs express an opinion and try to convince, or persuade, the readers that this opinion is correct.

Lesson 1.29 Writing a Paragraph

Match It
Circle the letter of the best answer in each of the following questions.

1. Which of the following sentences makes the best topic sentence?
   a. Pat was on a journey.
   b. Pat started on his journey with only his pack on his back.
   c. Pat had a backpack.

2. Which of the following topic sentences is the beginning of a descriptive paragraph?
   a. The day started out bright and sunny.
   b. School cafeterias should be open before and after school hours.
   c. Building a bookcase can be fast and easy.

3. Which of the following sentences is a sentence from the middle of a paragraph?
   a. A recycling program should be started in our school for three reasons.
   b. Recycling helps the environment.
   c. Recycling will benefit us all.

4. Which of the following sentences is from a narrative paragraph?
   a. The bears can weigh up to 800 pounds.
   b. Littering is unsanitary and inconsiderate.
   c. Pat journeyed many days and many nights.

Try It
Write a short descriptive, narrative, expository, or persuasive paragraph. After you have chosen your topic, use the first section to write a rough draft of your paragraph. Use the second section to rewrite your paragraph with all corrections and revisions made.

_____

_____

_____

_____

_____

_____

_____

_____

_____

_____

Review Chapter 1 Lessons 20–29

Review: Declarative Sentences, Interrogative Sentences, Exclamatory Sentences, Imperative Sentences

Putting It Together
Identify the following sentences. After each sentence, write if the sentence is *declarative*, *interrogative*, *exclamatory*, or *imperative*.

1. Walk up the steps and then turn left. _____

2. Anne took a risk and accepted the new job. _____

3. Was that statue priceless? _____

4. Our team won the game in the final two seconds! _____

Review: Simple Sentences, Compound Sentences, Complex Sentences, Sentence Fragments, Combining Sentences

After each sentence, write whether it is a *simple sentence*, a *compound sentence*, a *complex sentence*, or a *sentence fragment*. If the sentences are simple sentences or sentence fragments, rewrite them as compound or complex.

1. Edward and Cynthia wrapped and delivered the presents. _____

   _____

2. Although it was a sunny day, _____

   _____

3. The coach challenged her team. The coach inspired her team. _____

   _____

4. Grill the peaches until they are slightly brown. _____

   _____

5. The ocean was blue. The ocean was warm. _____

   _____

6. After the hike, _____

   _____

Review Chapter 1 Lessons 20–29

The following paragraph is out of order. Reorder the sentences so they make sense. Rewrite the paragraph and then write what kind of paragraph it is.

It also protects our natural habitats. We should all be committed to a recycling program. The same is true with curbside pollution; less trash means less trash and pollution on our streets. Recycling greatly reduces our need for landfills. It also reduces curbside pollution. When we cut down trees, birds, squirrels, rabbits, and many other forest animals lose their homes. Recycling is important to our environment for many reasons. These are excellent reasons why we should encourage our friends and family to recycle. If we recycle the paper products we use, fewer trees will have to be cut down. Recycling saves trees. If we recycle what would be trash, there will be less garbage to put into the landfills.

_____

_____

_____

_____

_____

_____

_____

_____

_____

_____

_____

_____

_____

_____

_____

_____

Chapter 2
Lesson 2.1 Proper Nouns: Cities, States, Countries

NAME _____

The names of cities, states, and countries are considered **proper nouns** and are always capitalized.

Capitalize the names of cities:
      Anchorage   Columbus   Kona   Detroit   Los Angeles   New York

Capitalize the names of states:
      Alaska   Ohio   Hawaii   Michigan   California   New York

Capitalize the names of countries:
      United States   Mexico   Japan   Denmark   Israel

Do not capitalize the words *city*, *state*, or *country* in a sentence. These words are common nouns.

Complete It
Circle the correct answer in each of the following sentences.

1. The capital of California is (Sacramento, sacramento).
2. This (City, city) has a population of approximately 407,000.
3. (Los Angeles, los Angeles), has the largest population in California.
4. The city in the United States with the largest population is (New York, new york).
5. The (City, city) of New York has a population of approximately 22 million.
6. The capital city of the state of (New York, new york) is Albany.
7. Albany, (New York, new york) has a population of approximately 40,800.
8. The largest city in (California, california) is Los Angeles.
9. California is the most populated (State, state) in the United States.
10. The least populated state in the United States is (Wyoming, wyoming).
11. China is the most populated (Country, country).
12. The population of (China, china) is over 1.2 billion.
13. The population of the (United States, united States) is over 293 million.
14. The largest continent, Asia, is made up of 48 (Countries, countries).
15. Australia is the only continent that is its own (Country, country).

Lesson 2.1 Proper Nouns: Cities, States, Countries

Proof It
Proofread the following journal entry. Use the proofreading marks to correct capitalization errors.

EIFFEL TOWER

≡ – capitalizes a letter
/ – lowercases a letter

Today was my fourth day in Europe. We have been

traveling quickly. I feel like I'm a long way from my home in

athens, Ohio. We started our trip in London, england. We saw Big Ben and the Tower of

London. Then we took the tube to paris, france. We climbed the Eiffel Tower – what an

awesome view! We also saw the Mona Lisa at The Louvre Museum. France is a

beautiful Country. Then it was off to belgium. We started our tour in the City of Brugges.

I have eaten many waffles in ohio, but I've never seen as many as in this Country.

Tomorrow we leave belgium for munich, germany. I'm hoping to eat one of those big

pretzels while I'm there. I know next year I'm taking an eating tour of Europe.

Try It
Write a journal entry about a city you have visited. Be sure to name the state, if it applies, and the country.

_____

_____

_____

_____

_____

_____

_____

_____

Lesson 2.2 Proper Nouns: Days of the Week, Months of the Year

Days of the week and months of the year are considered **proper nouns** and are always capitalized.

Capitalize days of the week:

Sunday   Monday   Tuesday   Wednesday   Thursday   Friday   Saturday

Capitalize months of the year:

January   February   March   April   May   June
July   August   September   October   November   December

Solve It

The following sentences each contain the name of a day of the week. However, the sentences don't make sense. Unscramble the names of the days of the week so the sentences make sense. Write the day on the line after each sentence. Remember to capitalize the day of the week.

1. dswdeayen falls in the middle of the week. _____

2. The day ryifda got its name from the German word *frigga*. _____

3. The sun gave its name to nysuda. _____

4. hsruydta was named for Thor, a god in northern mythology. _____

5. On onmayd, the day of the moon, I go to school. _____

6. I play baseball on suartyad, the first day of the weekend. _____

7. Tiw's day gives its name to usedtay, honoring the northern mythological wrestler Tir. _____

January						
1	2	3	4	5	6	7
8	9	10	11	12	13	14
15	16	17	18	19	20	21
22	23	24	25	26	27	28
29	30	31				

February						
		1	2	3	4	
5	6	7	8	9	10	11
12	13	14	15	16	17	18
19	20	21	22	23	24	25
26	27	28				

March						
		1	2	3	4	
5	6	7	8	9	10	11
12	13	14	15	16	17	18
19	20	21	22	23	24	25
26	27	28	29	30	31	

April						
						1
2	3	4	5	6	7	8
9	10	11	12	13	14	15
16	17	18	19	20	21	22
23	24	25	26	27	28	29
30						

May						
	1	2	3	4	5	6
7	8	9	10	11	12	13
14	15	16	17	18	19	20
21	22	23	24	25	26	27
28	29	30	31			

June						
				1	2	3
4	5	6	7	8	9	10
11	12	13	14	15	16	17
18	19	20	21	22	23	24
25	26	27	28	29	30	

July						
						1
2	3	4	5	6	7	8
9	10	11	12	13	14	15
16	17	18	19	20	21	22
23	24	25	26	27	28	29
30	31					

August						
	1	2	3	4	5	
6	7	8	9	10	11	12
13	14	15	16	17	18	19
20	21	22	23	24	25	26
27	28	29	30	31		

September						
					1	2
3	4	5	6	7	8	9
10	11	12	13	14	15	16
17	18	19	20	21	22	23
24	25	26	27	28	29	30

October						
1	2	3	4	5	6	7
8	9	10	11	12	13	14
15	16	17	18	19	20	21
22	23	24	25	26	27	28
29	30	31				

November						
			1	2	3	4
5	6	7	8	9	10	11
12	13	14	15	16	17	18
19	20	21	22	23	24	25
26	27	28	29	30		

December						
					1	2
3	4	5	6	7	8	9
10	11	12	13	14	15	16
17	18	19	20	21	22	23
24	25	26	27	28	29	30
31						

Lesson 2.2 Proper Nouns: Days of the Week, Months of the Year

Complete It

Complete the following sentences by writing the correct month of the year on the line. Remember to capitalize the month when you write it in. Use an encyclopedia or the Internet if you need help.

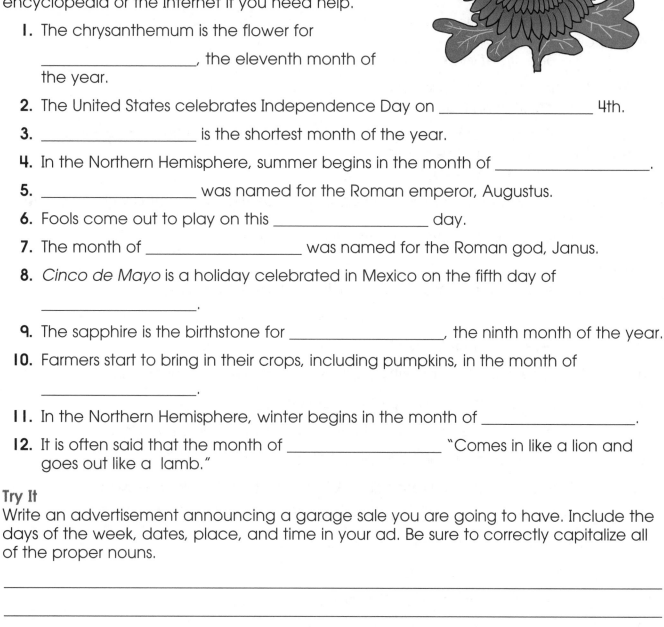

1. The chrysanthemum is the flower for

   _____, the eleventh month of the year.

2. The United States celebrates Independence Day on _____ 4th.

3. _____ is the shortest month of the year.

4. In the Northern Hemisphere, summer begins in the month of _____.

5. _____ was named for the Roman emperor, Augustus.

6. Fools come out to play on this _____ day.

7. The month of _____ was named for the Roman god, Janus.

8. *Cinco de Mayo* is a holiday celebrated in Mexico on the fifth day of

   _____.

9. The sapphire is the birthstone for _____, the ninth month of the year.

10. Farmers start to bring in their crops, including pumpkins, in the month of

    _____.

11. In the Northern Hemisphere, winter begins in the month of _____.

12. It is often said that the month of _____ "Comes in like a lion and goes out like a lamb."

Try It

Write an advertisement announcing a garage sale you are going to have. Include the days of the week, dates, place, and time in your ad. Be sure to correctly capitalize all of the proper nouns.

_____

_____

_____

_____

_____

Lesson 2.3 Proper Nouns: Names of Streets, Places, People

The names of specific streets, places, and people are proper nouns and are capitalized.

Capitalize the names of specific streets.

    Stanley Street   Ohio Avenue   Crosswinds Boulevard

When using the nonspecific words like *street* and *road* in a sentence, they are not capitalized.

    I live one *street* over from you.

Capitalize the names of specific places.
    Rocky Mountain National Park

Capitalize the first and last names of people, including special titles, initials, and abbreviations that go with the names.
    President Jimmy Carter

Do not capitalize nonspecific street names, places, or titles when used without a name in a sentence.
    My best friend is going to run for class president.

Identify It
Write **PN** if the sentence has a proper noun. If not, leave it blank.

1. _____ Felicia and Bryan stayed at the Lake Hotel on their vacation.

2. _____ Drive slowly on this street, many children play here.

3. _____ Dr. Edwards gave my kitty a pill that will make her feel better.

4. _____ The hotel where we stayed was beautiful.

5. _____ Cross over Breeze Loop and then turn right on Riverbend Drive.

6. _____ The president of our class will speak at the rally.

7. _____ Hawaii Volcanoes National Park is located on the island Hawaii.

8. _____ The park has many attractions.

9. _____ The doctor was kind to her patients.

10. _____ Karl lives on Lane Road.

11. _____ The bridge connected Mill Drive to Shamrock Road.

12. _____ Dr. Green is a wonderful veterinarian.

Lesson 2.3 Proper Nouns: Names of Streets, Places, People

Proofread the following paragraph using proofreading marks.
Look for errors in the use of capitalization with proper nouns.

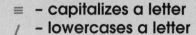

≡ – capitalizes a letter
/ – lowercases a letter

    Do you believe in haunted houses? How about haunted hotels? Granville, Ohio is home to the buxton inn. The buxton inn, located on broadway street, has a haunting reputation. The Hotel was built in 1812 by orrin granger, founder of the City of Granville. The Hotel was named after major buxton, who ran the inn from 1865–1905. So who's ghost has appeared in this Inn? orrin granger was first seen in the 1920s eating a piece of pie in the kitchen. major buxton has been seen by Guests, mostly in the Dining Room. The ghosts of other Owner's have also been spotted. Even a kitty of days gone by has been seen roaming throughout the buxton inn. Of course the ghost cat now has a name – Major Buxton.

Try It
Write a short autobiography. Write about the city where you were born, the name of the first street where you lived, your parents' and siblings' names, and the name of your first school and first teacher. Write about a few of your favorite memories growing up. Make sure all of the proper nouns in your autobiography are capitalized.

_____

_____

_____

_____

_____

_____

_____

_____

_____

_____

Lesson 2.4 Proper Nouns: Words Used as Names, Official Names

Words like *mother*, *father*, *aunt*, and *uncle* can be used as **proper nouns** or **common nouns**. When they are used as proper nouns, they should be capitalized.

The words *mother* and *father* can be used in place of name. If they are, they are capitalized.

> *Mother*, where did I leave my jacket?

In the following instance, *father* is not used as a replacement of a name.

> My *father* took me to the hockey game.

The same is true for the words *aunt, uncle, grandmother,* and *grandfather*.

> *Aunt Clara* has a wonderful cat.
> My *aunt* likes to travel in the mountains.
> I like to play catch with *Uncle Richard*.
> My *uncle* was great in sports when he was in school.

Official names, such as those of businesses and their products, are capitalized. Nonspecific names of products are not capitalized, even if they follow the business or product name.

> *Papa's Pizza* (name of business)
> I like *Papa's Pizza's* pizza. (business name followed by product name)

Match It
Circle the letter that matches the description.

1. the word *mother* not used to replace a name
   a. Mother, please pass the beans.
   b. My mother was the pitcher on her softball team.

2. the word *grandfather* used as a name
   a. Grandfather Clarence was a veterinarian.
   b. My grandfather is a good cook.

3. the word *aunt* not used to replace a name
   a. My aunt has the cutest puppy.
   b. Aunt Marilyn is a teacher.

4. official business name followed by product name
   a. Oat Crisps cereal
   b. Oat Crisps

5. official business name without product name
   a. Tender Pet pet food
   b. Tender Pet

Lesson 2.4 Proper Nouns: Words Used as Names, Official Names

Solve It

Fill in the missing information on this family tree. Be sure to capitalize proper names. Write three different sentences about the people on this tree.

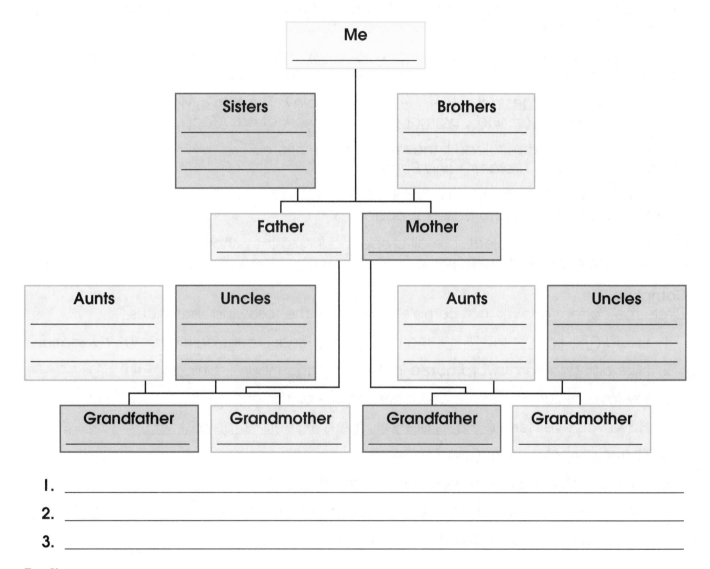

1. _____

2. _____

3. _____

Try It

What products would you like to invent? Invent some products of your own. Then, give your products an official business name. Come up with at least three business names and three product names. Be sure to capitalize the official business names.

1. _____

2. _____

3. _____

Lesson 2.5 Proper Nouns: Titles, Names of Subjects

Titles are **proper nouns** and are capitalized. The first and last words of titles are always capitalized, as well as every word in between except for articles (*a, an, the*), short prepositions (*in, of, at*), and short conjunctions (*and, but*). These words, however, should be capitalized if they are the first word in the title. Most titles are also underlined in text. Song titles and essays, however, are in quotes.

This rule applies to titles of the following: books, newspapers, magazines, articles, poems, songs, plays, movies, works of art, pictures, stories, and essays.

book: *Catcher in the Rye*   play: *The Music Man*
movie: *Master and Commander*   work of art: *Mona Lisa*

School subjects are capitalized if they name a specific course.
My favorite course is *Literature and Poetry*.

Do not capitalize the names of general subjects.
My *math* teacher is also the baseball coach.

Exception: Language subjects are all proper nouns, so they should all be capitalized.
I am studying my *French* homework.

Complete It
Circle the correct answer that completes each of the following sentences.

1. I read (The Lord of the Rings, the Lord Of The Rings) series during summer vacation.

2. I like doing the crossword puzzle in the (Chicago tribune, Chicago Tribune).

3. My favorite song is ("Drops of Jupiter", "drops of jupiter").

4. Have you ever seen (Raiders of The lost Ark, Raiders of the Lost Ark)?

5. I have gym class after (spanish, Spanish).

6. Mr. Howard is the best (history, History) teacher.

7. Mr. Hayes teaches a course called (Geometry, geometry).

8. Can I walk with you to (Math, math) class?

9. My sister is studying (American poetry, american poetry) in college.

10. The poem ("Dawn", "dawn") by Paul Lawrence Dunbar is one of Dylan's favorites.

Lesson 2.5 Proper Nouns: Titles, Names of Subjects

Rewrite It
These reviews have errors in capitalization. Make the corrections as you rewrite them.

* Sleeper of the Year! The movie <u>Happy Times In Snoozeville</u> is for you if you need a nap. The dialogue is boring, the action is slow, and the actors can't act. Don't waste your money on this dud.

* Great Read! The <u>perfect Peach</u> is just what it says—a peach. Take this book to the beach or read it in your favorite armchair. The <u>perfect Peach</u> has rich characters and a comforting mood. Don't miss this great read.

* Ouch! My Ears! What was Kay Joe thinking when she recorded "Dancing in the desert"? She can't hit the high notes and the lyrics make no sense. The track "Singing On The Seas" is worth the money—but buy the single.

_____

_____

_____

_____

_____

_____

_____

_____

_____

_____

Try It
Write the title of your favorites below. Don't forget to capitalize when necessary and underline or use quotes correctly.

book _____   magazine _____

movie _____   poem _____

song _____   play _____

Lesson 2.6 Sentences, Direct Quotations

The first word of every **sentence** is capitalized.
Build the parfait by sprinkling the berries on the yogurt.

The first word in **direct quotations** is capitalized. Quotation marks are used to show the exact words of a speaker, a direct quotation. The quotation marks are placed before and after the exact words.

Our teacher said, "*Please* go to the board and write your answer."
"*I* hope I know the answer," I whispered as I walked to the board.

Indirect quotations are not capitalized. An indirect quotation does not use the exact words of a speaker and does not use quotation marks.
The coach said he wanted to have practice three nights a week.

If a quotation is split and the second half continues, do not capitalize the second half. If a new sentence begins after the split, then capitalize it as you would with any sentence.
"I think my puppy is the cutest in the class," said the boy, "*and* the best trained."
"My aunt took me to the shelter to get a kitty," said Candy. "*We* found the perfect calico!"

Identify It

One of the sentences in each of the following pairs is not capitalized correctly. Write an **X** on the line before the sentence that is capitalized correctly.

1. _____ The apartment was perfect for Phyllis and Marc.

   _____ the apartment was perfect for Phyllis and Marc.

2. _____ "Check out the exercise room," said Maria. "It has everything we use."

   _____ "Check out the exercise room," said Maria. "it has everything we use."

3. _____ The agent John said The pool will open in the spring.

   _____ The agent John said the pool will open in the spring.

4. _____ "Rob," said Regina, "the view is fantastic!"

   _____ "Rob," said Regina, "The view is fantastic!"

5. _____ Eddy and Jackie decided They would move next month.

   _____ Eddy and Jackie decided they would move next month.

NAME _____

Lesson 2.6 Sentences, Direct Quotations

Use the proofreading marks to correct the errors in capitalization.

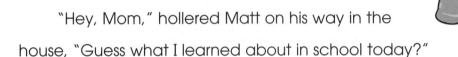

> ≡ - capitalizes a letter
> / - lowercases a letter

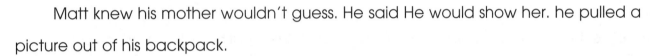

"Hey, Mom," hollered Matt on his way in the

house, "Guess what I learned about in school today?"

Matt knew his mother wouldn't guess. He said He would show her. he pulled a

picture out of his backpack.

"Here it is, Mom," said Matt. "it's a snot otter!"

"Oh my," exclaimed his mom, "What exactly is a snot otter?"

"I knew you would ask," Matt gleefully replied. "snot otters are a type of

salamander. they live in cool, fast moving streams with big rocks. They live up to 29

years. But their habitats are declining."

"That is sad," replied Matt's mother. "why are they in danger?"

"Water pollution and sediment build-up in streams are a couple of reasons they

are in danger," answered Matt. "if someone finds a snot otter, it should be put back in

the stream. They are not pets."

"Well, I'm glad to hear that," Matt's mom said smiling.

Try It
Write a dialogue about a student telling a teacher about an animal. Pay attention to
the capitalization of sentences in and outside of dialogue.

_____

_____

_____

_____

_____

Lesson 2.7 Personal Letters

A **personal letter** has five parts: heading, salutation, body, closing, and signature. Personal letters have special punctuation.

The **heading** of a personal letter is the address of the person writing the letter and the date it is written. The name of the street, city, state, and month are all capitalized.

> 3126 Milly Dr.
> Marblehead, MI 20000
> October 5, 2006

The **salutation** is the greeting and begins with *dear*. Both *dear* and the name of the person who is receiving the letter are capitalized. Place a comma after the name.

> Dear Stanley,

The **body** is the main part of the letter and is capitalized just like all sentences and paragraphs.

The **closing** can be written many ways. Only the first word is capitalized. Place a comma after the closing.

> Your friend,   Sincerely,   All the best,

The **signature** is usually only your first name. It is always capitalized.

> Milton

Proof It
Proofread the personal letter. Use the proofreading marks to make corrections in capitalization.

≡	– capitalizes a letter
/	– lowercases a letter

5711 eastwind loop
anchorage, AK 20000
february 26, 2008

dear aunt Linda,

How have you been? I've been great. school is going very well this year. I really like social studies and english. However I've had a little trouble with math. my best friend is helping me with that.

I'm playing on the junior varsity basketball team. I love it. I think I will try out for the track team this spring.

I can't wait to see you on your next visit. Please tell uncle Ray I said hello.

With Love,
Kay

Lesson 2.7 Personal Letters

Try It
Write a personal letter. Be sure to capitalize the letter correctly. Use the information provided on page 80 if you need help setting your personal letter up correctly.

_____

_____

_____

_____

_____

_____

_____

_____

_____

_____

_____

_____

_____

_____

_____

_____

_____

_____

_____

_____

_____

_____

_____

_____

_____

_____

Review Chapter 2 Lessons 1-7

Review: Proper Nouns: Cities, States, Countries, Days of the Week, Months of the Year, Names of Streets, Places, People, Words Used as Names, Official Names, Titles, Names of Subjects, Sentences, Direct Quotations, Personal Letters

Putting It Together
Proofread the following personal letter. Make all of the necessary capitalization corrections. Then, use the following page to rewrite the letter.

≡	– capitalizes a letter
/	– lowercases a letter

4064 palm tree lane

oakdale, FL 20000

March 19, 2008

dear Perry,

How do you like anaheim, california? Do you like your new school? things are about the same here. I'm getting ready for the baseball season. Our first game is next thursday. coach Baum says That I can start as pitcher.

The basketball team won the division, but we didn't get very far in state. I think the baseball team will do well. we already have a sponsor for the team. Fast Feet Sporting Goods has already signed on. I like Fast Feet Shoes, but I'm still going to buy my gloves from your Uncle's store.

My family is going on vacation this summer. We're going to chicago, illinois. My Grandpa and Grandma are going, too. We are going to visit aunt Christina. We're also going to the navy pier and the sears tower. Did you know that the Sears Tower used to be the tallest Building in the world?

Are you trying out for the track team this year? Aren't try-outs in march? I hope you get to come back to visit soon. maybe we can meet somewhere in the middle next winter break? Write when you can.

your Friend,

Denny

Review Chapter 2 Lessons 1-7

Lesson 2.8 Periods: After Declarative and Imperative Sentences, In Dialogue

Declarative and imperative sentences both use **periods**. A declarative sentence makes a statement. An imperative sentence demands an action be performed, and the subject is usually not expressed. Sometimes, an imperative sentence can end with an exclamation point.

> They left for their trip on Friday.
> Look at the icicle formations on the roof!

Quotation marks are used to set off direct quotations in dialogue. Quotation marks are placed before and after the direct quotation. A period is placed at the end of a direct quotation sentence when it is declarative or imperative. The period goes inside the quotation mark.

> Lori said, "I'll give the ticket to the agent."

In direct quotation sentences when the quote comes at the beginning of the sentence, use a comma at the end of the direct quotation instead of a period.

> "I'll give the ticket to the agent," said Lori.

Complete It
Add the correct punctuation mark in each sentence.

1. "My house is on the right__" said Martha.

2. Martha said__ "My house is on the right."

3. "Look at the bright plants my mom planted__"

4. "My house has plants like that__" Deidre replied.

5. Deidre continued, "We also have some bushes mixed in, too__"

Lesson 2.8 Periods: After Declarative and Imperative Sentences, In Dialogue

Proof It
Proofread the following paragraphs. Use proofreading marks to make punctuation corrections.

ℓ – **deletes letters, words, punctuation**
^ – **inserts letters, words, punctuation**

"Cities, like cats, reveal themselves at night" said the British poet Rupert Brooke. Perhaps he didn't realize how true his statement is Some cats save their owners' lives when they reveal themselves at night.

Take, for example, Aggie Aggie was a cat rescued from a shelter when she was five weeks old. Aggie was curious and playful, but not aggressive That is until one evening when she heard an intruder trying to climb through the front window Before her owners even made it downstairs, she pounced, attacked, and scared away the intruder.

Cats also rescue and save their own. One particular cat lived in an abandoned building with her five recently born kittens When the building caught on fire what was she to do? Of course she had to save her family. One by one she carried her kittens out of the burning building to safety. She was burned and blistered but she got every one of her kittens out The firefighter who made sure the cat and kittens were safe and cared for is now known as "The Animal Guy."

Try It
Interview a friend about his or her pet. Then, write a newspaper article about it. Be sure to include direct quotations.

_____

_____

_____

_____

_____

Lesson 2.9 Periods: In Abbreviations, In Initials, Titles Before Names

The **period** is used in more than just sentences. Periods are used in abbreviations, initials, and titles before names.

Use a period after each part of an abbreviation. Do not leave a space between the period and the following letter.

    B.C.   A.D.   B.A.

Use a period after each letter of an initial.

    Michael J. Fox   J. K. Rowling   J. R. R. Tolkien

Use a period with abbreviated titles before names.

    Dr.   Mr.   Mrs.

Do not use periods if the abbreviation is an acronym. **Acronyms** are words formed from the first letters of words in a phrase.

    NATO (North Atlantic Treaty Organization)

Match It

Draw a line to match the following abbreviations, titles, and acronyms in Column A with their meanings in Column B.

Column A	Column B
B.S.	Public Broadcasting System
DJ	United Nations International Children's Education Fund
PBS	District Attorney
D.A.	Disc Jockey
SCUBA	Mister
D.V.M.	Doctor of Veterinary Medicine
UNICEF	Bachelor of Science
Mr.	Self-contained underwater breathing apparatus
M.D.	Bachelor of Arts
B.A.	Medical Doctor

Lesson 2.9 Periods: In Abbreviations, In Initials, Titles Before Names

Rewrite It

The following people were either misidentified or are not pleased with how their names appeared in a recent magazine article. Rewrite them as they request.

I. Donna Kay Dell   "I prefer my middle name to be an initial."

_____

2. Melissa Sarah Oliver   "I prefer first and middle initials."

_____

3. Dr. E. Bates, Ph.D.   "I am a medical doctor."

_____

4. M. L. Roberts   "I am a doctor."

_____

5. Steven Paul Starks   "I would like my first name as an initial."

_____

Try It

You are having a formal party. Make a formal list of ten people you would like to invite. Include their titles and abbreviations, like Mr., Dr., Mrs., and M.D.

_____   _____

_____   _____

_____   _____

_____   _____

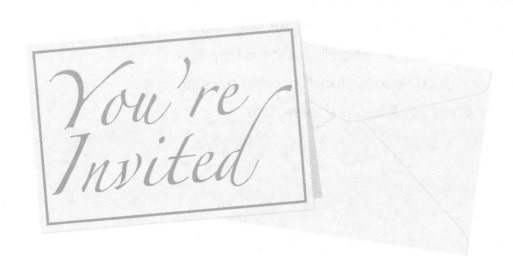

Lesson 2.10 Question Marks

Interrogative sentences ask questions and they are followed by **question marks**.
> How many students are in the class**?**

When used in quotations, questions marks can be placed either inside or outside of the end quotation mark depending on the meaning of the sentence.

When the question mark is punctuating the quotation itself, it is placed inside the quote.
> The customer asked, "How much does the car cost**?**"

When the question mark is punctuating the entire sentence, it is placed outside the quote.
> Did the sales person say, "It's the most expensive car on the lot"**?**

A question mark is unnecessary in sentences with indirect quotations.
> I asked my sister if she would help us with our math homework.

Complete It

Place a question mark in the appropriate place in the sentences that need one. In the sentences that do not use a question mark, place a period at the end of the sentence.

1. Did you hear back from the admission's office

2. Jason said he saw the movie 12 times

3. My mom asked, "How much homework do you have tonight"

4. Did your teacher say, "Finish the entire chapter tonight"

5. I asked Jill if she had a good day

6. There must have been 200 people in the theatre

7. The hiker asked, "Is this as far as this trail goes"

8. The server asked if we wanted dessert

9. Are you going to play tennis with your sister this evening

10. Dr. Eric said to take the medicine once a day

11. My brother asked, "Is Judy studying with you after school"

12. Did the coach say, "Run three more laps"

Lesson 2.10 Question Marks

Proof It

Proofread the following dialogue. Make corrections using proofreading marks. Look for errors with question mark use.

 – **deletes letters, words, punctuation**
∧ – **inserts letters, words, punctuation**
⌣ – **moves punctuation from one place to another**

Patrick was doing a report on the Milky Way Galaxy. He asked the director of the local observatory if he could ask him some questions?

Patrick asked, "How many planets orbit the sun in our solar system"?

The director answered, "We have nine planets that orbit the sun."

Patrick asked, "Was my teacher right when she said planets are divided into two categories?"

"Yes, Patrick, Mrs. Sanchez was right," said the director. "Mercury, Venus, Earth, and Mars belong to the terrestrial planets." The director asked, "Do you know the name of the other category"?

"The other category is the Jovian planets?" answered Patrick.

The director said, "You are correct!"

Patrick had a good time and learned a lot about the Milky Way Galaxy. He asked the director if he could come back again?

Try It

Choose a subject you would like to know more about. Write a dialogue between you and your teacher. Ask your teacher questions about the subject you chose. Have your teacher ask you questions in the dialogue, too.

_____

_____

_____

_____

_____

Lesson 2.11 Exclamation Points

Exclamatory sentences are sentences that express surprise and strong emotion and are punctuated with **exclamation points**.

I'm so excited you made it into the first college on your list**!**

Interjections sometimes require exclamation points.

Oh, no**!** I left my homework at home!

Identify It

Identify which sentences should have exclamation points. Place an **X** at the end of each sentence that needs an exclamation point.

1. Watch out The stove is hot _____

2. The soup should be on medium high _____

3. Thank you for my beautiful flowers _____

4. Tulips are my favorite flower _____

5. Ouch My fingers were still in the door _____

6. After all my hard work, I finally got an A on the test _____

7. I have a lot of homework to do tonight _____

8. I won the race _____

9. Oh, no The rain is coming down really hard now _____

10. I like the sound of rain on the rooftop _____

11. The cars are coming fast _____

12. My favorite color is green _____

13. The ice is slippery _____

14. Don't shut the door before getting your keys _____

15. Wait I forgot the keys _____

Lesson 2.11 Exclamation Points

Solve It

Which of the following situations would require an exclamation point? Write a short sentence for each illustration you see. Include interjections and exclamation points when you think they are necessary.

_____

_____

_____

Try It

Write six more sentences that should be written using exclamation points.

1. _____

2. _____

3. _____

4. _____

5. _____

6. _____

Lesson 2.12 Commas: Series, Direct Address, Multiple Adjectives

Commas have a variety of uses. Three uses for commas are commas in a series, commas in direct address, and commas used with multiple adjectives.

A **series** is at least three items listed in a sentence in a row. The items can be words, phrases, or clauses. Commas are used to separate them.

> I must clean the *kitchen, the bathroom, and the family room* this weekend.

When the name of a person spoken to is used in a sentence, it is called **direct address**. A comma is used to separate the name of the person from the rest of the sentence.

> *Sarah,* after our chores are done, we can go to the park.

When more than one adjective is used to describe a noun, they are separated by commas.

> The *sweet, cool apple* tasted good on the hot day.

Make sure each adjective describes the noun. There is no comma in the following sentence because the pizza is not piping. The adverb *piping* describes the adjective *hot*.

> The *piping hot* pizza was ready to come out of the oven

Match It

Match the following sentences in Column A to the type of commas they require in Column B. Draw a line from Column A to Column B to make the match.

Column A	Column B
1. The soft, sweet, loving kitten purred.	commas in a series
2. They stayed out of the biting cold water.	commas in direct address
3. Daphne, please answer the door.	commas separating adjectives
4. I worked out on the treadmill, bike, and elliptical cycle.	no comma necessary

Column A	Column B
5. The sizzling hot sauce was too hot to eat.	commas in a series
6. Stephanie, please pass the strawberries.	commas in direct address
7. The sweet, juicy, ripe peaches were perfect.	commas separating adjectives
8. The tennis players grabbed their towels, bags, and balls on their way off the court.	no comma necessary

Lesson 2.12 Commas: Series, Direct Address, Multiple Adjectives

Rewrite It

Rewrite the sentences, adding commas where necessary.

1. John wanted pasta vegetables and rolls for dinner.

   _____

2. Tiffany make the reservation for 7:30.

   _____

3. The new black car was just what he wanted.

   _____

4. I checked in on the slowly boiling water.

   _____

5. Keith had to do his homework eat dinner and take out the trash.

   _____

Try It

Make a list of five of your favorite things. Then, make a list of words that describe these things. Write five sentences about your favorite things using the words that describe them. Be sure to include commas in the appropriate places.

1. _____   _____

   _____

2. _____   _____

   _____

3. _____   _____

   _____

4. _____   _____

   _____

5. _____   _____

   _____

Lesson 2.13 Commas: Combining Sentences, Set-Off Dialogue

Use a **comma** to combine two independent clauses with a coordinate conjunction.
The players must be well trained, *and* they must train for at least six months.

If a sentence begins with a prepositional phrase, set it off with a comma.
After he finishes his homework, he can talk with his friends.

Commas are also used when setting off dialogue from the rest of the sentence.
The tour guide said, *"Today's walking tour will take us past several museums."*
"Then, we will eat in a cafe," promised the tour guide.

Complete It

Complete the following sentences by adding commas where necessary. Not all of the sentences need commas.

1. The Teton Mountain Range is a beautiful sight and it is a challenge for rock climbers.

2. The Teton Mountain Range is located in Wyoming and the range is in part of the Grand Teton National Park.

3. Because of its beauty more than 3 million people visit each year.

4. Visitors have been known to say "This is one of the most inspiring places I've seen."

5. Millions of people gaze at the peaks yet it remains peaceful.

6. The range not only has more than 100 lakes but also 200 miles of trails.

7. Rock climbers come from all over the world to climb Grand Teton.

8. "The view from the mountain is breathtaking" said one climber.

9. While Grand Teton's highest peek is 13,700 feet other peaks attract climbers.

10. "Wildlife viewing is amazing here" said another tourist.

Lesson 2.13 Commas: Combining Sentences, Set-Off Dialogue

Proof It
Proofread the following paragraph. Add commas where necessary.

> – deletes letters, words, punctuation
> ∧ – inserts letters, words, punctuation

What is a marathon? Most runners know that a marathon is a foot race of 26.2 miles but not everyone knows how the marathon began. Now popular worldwide the marathon has its roots in Greece. We are familiar with bicycle couriers but ancient Greeks used foot couriers. Many of them had to run city to city to make deliveries. In 490 B.C. Persia was at war with Greece. A Persian army landed 25 miles from Athens at the city of Marathon. After a mighty battle the Greeks were victorious. A runner was sent from Marathon to Athens to spread the news of the victory. Pheidippides ran the 25 miles from Marathon to Athens. When he reached the city legend says he said "Rejoice, we conquer." Then, Pheidippides fell dead. Although the facts are not known for sure the legend prevails. The modern race got a name and the marathon was born.

Try It
Write a paragraph explaining your favorite sport, how it got its beginning, and why you like it. Use a variety of sentences. Add a quotation of your own.

_____

_____

_____

_____

_____

_____

_____

_____

Lesson 2.14 Commas: Personal Letters

The five parts of the personal letter are: **heading, salutation (greeting), body, closing,** and **signature. Commas** appear in four of the five parts of the personal letter.

A **comma** follows the city and the date in the heading.

> 3151 Stuckey Lane
> Chicago, IL 30000
> March 7, 2008

A **comma** follows the name in the salutation.

> Dear Mary,

Follow the normal rules for using comma in sentences.

A **comma** follows the last word in the closing.

> Your friend,

⬆ - inserts commas

Proof It
Proof the following friendly letter. Add commas where necessary.

> 5512 Alpine Lane
>
> Ridgeview CO 55214
>
> April 26 2008
>
> Dear Marina
>
> How are you? Are you getting excited for summer? I am going to volunteer at the local animal shelter and I am going to learn all about the different kinds of animals there. I am sure that it will be a hard job but it will be rewarding, too.
>
> What are your plans for summer? Will you be going camping with your parents like you did last year? That sounds like so much fun! After you get back I want to know all about it.
>
> I need to get back to reading about animal care and I hope to hear from you soon!
>
> Your friend
>
> Sharon

Lesson 2.14 Commas: Personal Letters

Try It

Write a friendly letter of your own. Pay attention to your use of commas.

_____

_____

_____

_____

_____

_____

_____

_____

_____

_____

_____

_____

_____

_____

_____

_____

_____

_____

_____

_____

_____

_____

_____

_____

_____

_____

Lesson 2.15 Quotation Marks

Quotation marks are used to show the exact words of a speaker, called a **direct quotation**. The quotation marks are placed before and after the exact words.

"I must make it to the post office before 5:00," said Sharon. "I want to get my invitations in the mail today."

Quotation marks are also used when a direct quotation is made within a direct quotation. In this case, single quotation marks are used to set off the inside quotation.

Dylan said, "Michael, the coach said, 'Practice will be at 4:00 instead of 3:00.'"

The single quotation marks express what the coach said. The double quotation marks express what Dylan is saying as a direct quote.

Quotation marks are used with some titles. Quotation marks are used with the titles of short stories, poems, songs, and articles in magazines and newspapers.

short story: "*A White Heron*"

If a title is quoted within a direct quotation, then single quotation marks are used.

Hannah said, "I hope the DJ plays my favorite song, 'Purple People Eater.'"

Match It

Match the following sentences or titles from Column A to the type of quotation in Column B. Draw a line to make the match.

Column A	Column B
1. Susan said, "Let's go to lunch at 12:30."	direct quotation
2. "Prairie Island," Connie answered. "My boss said, 'Our lunch meeting is scheduled for 12:00 sharp.'"	quote within a quote
	title
3. "Prairie Island"	

Column A	Column B
4. "Soak Up the Sun"	direct quotation
5. My sister said, "The coach said 'Eat a good dinner the night before the game.'"	quote within a quote
	title
6. "I'm heading for the beach," Sheryl said.	

Lesson 2.15 Quotation Marks

Proof It
Proofread the following dialogue using proofreading marks. Make corrections on the use of quotation marks.

˅ - inserts quotations

Claude Monet lived from 1840 to 1926. He was the founder of impressionism, said Mrs. Konikow.

What is impressionism? asked Doug.

Impressionism is an art form that captures a visual image and uses colors to give the effect of reflected light. Many of Monet's paintings were landscapes, answered Mrs. Konikow.

"Did Mrs. Konikow say, Many of Monet's paintings were landscapes?" asked Patricia.

Yes, answered Doug, landscapes are stretches of scenery that can be scene in one view.

Like flower gardens? asked Patricia.

Yes, Patricia, said Mrs. Konikow, like flower gardens. Later in his life, Monet retired from Paris and moved to his home in Giverny, France, where he continued to paint. He had beautiful gardens. You can see them in books and at his house in France.

Someday, I would like to go to France, said Patricia, but for now I think I'll just take a trip to the library.

Try It
Practice writing sentences with quotation marks. Write one sentence that is a direct quotation, one that is a quote within quotes, and one that includes a title.

1. _____

2. _____

3. _____

Lesson 2.16 Apostrophes

Apostrophes are used to form contractions, possessives, and plurals.

Contractions are shortened forms of words. The words are shorted by leaving out letters. An apostrophe takes the place of the omitted letters.

I am = I'm   *let us = let's*

Possessives show possession, or ownership. To form the possessive of a singular noun, add an apostrophe and an **s**.

I have *Walt's books*.

To form the possessive of plural nouns ending in **s**, simply add the apostrophe. If the plural noun does not end in an **s**, add both the apostrophe and an **s**.

The *boys' uniforms* will be ready on Friday.
The *children's puppet show* will be performed on Wednesday.

If you are writing about more than one letter of the alphabet or number, only add **s** to form the plural.

My name has two B**s** in it.
I have two page 4**s** in my book.

Complete It

Complete the following sentences by changing words to contractions. Write the contraction on the line that follows the words.

We're	It's	He'd
I'm	We've	let's

1. (I am) _____ hungry and thirsty.

2. (We are) _____ on our way to the café.

3. (It is) _____ not too far away, and it has the best muffins.

4. Do you think we should take something back for Pablo? (He would) _____ appreciate it.

5. (We have) _____ a lot of homework to do at lunch.

6. Come on, (let us) _____ hurry.

Lesson 2.16 Apostrophes

Solve It

Look at the pictures below and write a sentence for each that identifies the object and who the object belongs to. The first one has been done for you.

1. The children's toys are everywhere.

2. _____

3. _____

4. _____

5. _____

Try It

Write how many letters are duplicated in the following names. Then, on the last line, write your name. Write how many letters are duplicated in your name. The first one has been done for you.

1. Nathan 2 Ns and 2 As _____

2. Lee _____

3. Greg _____

5. David _____

4. Marjorie _____

6. _____

Lesson 2.17 Colons

Colons are used to introduce a series, to set off a clause, for emphasis, and in time.

Colons are used to introduce a series in a sentence. Usually, but not always, the list is proceeded by the words *following, these, things*.

> The chef does the *following:* washes the vegetables, chops the vegetables, and steams the vegetables.

Colons are sometimes used instead of a comma, in more formal cases, to set off a clause.

> The weather reporter said*: "We can expect six more inches of snow overnight."*

Colons are used to set off a word or phrase for emphasis.

> We hoped to see some activity in the night sky. And then we saw it*: a shooting star.*

Colons are used when writing the time.

> Are we meeting at *9:00* or *10:00*?

Identify It

Identify why the colon is used in each sentence. Write a **S** for series, **C** for clause, **E** for emphasis, or **T** for time.

1. _____ One of the most violent storms occurs primarily in the United States: tornados.

2. _____ A tornado is defined as the following: "a violent rotating column of air extending from a thunderstorm to the ground."

3. _____ Thunderstorms that develop in warm, moist air in advance of a cold front can produce these things: hail, strong wind, and tornados.

4. _____ Tornados are most likely to occur in the spring and summer months between 3:00pm and 9:00pm, but can occur anytime.

5. _____ Staying aware is most important for safety. During storms, look for the following: dark, greenish skies, large hail, loud roars, and flash floods.

6. _____ You can be prepared by doing the following: developing a safety plan, practicing house drills, and listening to weather reports.

Lesson 2.17 Colons

Rewrite It
Rewrite the following passage, adding colons where needed.

I would like to apply for the following position Latin Cultural Food Writer. I graduated from the Culinary Art Institute in New York. I have cooked dishes from many cultures Latin, French, and Middle Eastern.

I have expertise in Mexican food history, culture, and cooking. When the Spanish explorer Cortez first came to America he found many culinary surprises chocolate, peanuts, vanilla, beans, squash, avocados, coconuts, corn, and tomatoes. I have created many dishes which incorporate many of these foods and flavors.

Included with this letter are the following my resume, school transcripts, and references.

You can reach me weekdays between 7 00am and 3 00pm.

_____

_____

_____

_____

_____

_____

_____

_____

_____

_____

Try It
Write four sentences, one for each type of colon use: series, clause, emphasis, and time.

1. _____

2. _____

3. _____

4. _____

Lesson 2.18 Semicolons

A **semicolon** is a cross between a period and a comma. Semicolons can be used to join two independent clauses, to separate clauses containing commas, and to separate groups which contain commas.

Semicolons join two independent clauses when a coordinate conjunction is not used. The loud thunder scared me; I hid under my covers.

Semicolons are used to separate clauses when they already contain commas. Although the thunder was loud, it did no harm; I emerged from my bed safe and sound.

Semicolons are also used to separate words or phrases that already contain commas. We are looking for the following features in our new house: *a garage with space for two cars, storage, and tools; a kitchen with a refrigerator, dishwasher, stove, and microwave; and bedrooms with closets and a bathroom.*

Match It

Match the first half of the sentences in Column A with the second half in Column B. Then, circle all of the semicolons in the sentences.

Column A

1. Donna was close to home;

2. After the game was over, my team went for pizza;

3. The long shopping list included the following:

4. I didn't go to school;

5. Because we were on vacation, we weren't home to get the call;

6. Before sending the resume do the following:

Column B

I went to the doctor, instead.

it wasn't important anyway.

she had traveled a long way.

check the spelling, facts, and names; call your references; and verify the address.

we were all starving.

rye, pumpernickel, and wheat bread; lettuce, carrots, and onions for salad; and cranberry , grapefruit, and tomato juice.

Lesson 2.18 Semicolons

Proof It
Proofread the following magazine article using proofreading marks. Look for missing and out of place semicolons, and commas used instead of semicolons.

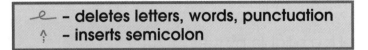

- *e* – **deletes letters, words, punctuation**
- ^ – **inserts semicolon**

Who is Sue? Sue is a Tyrannosaurus rex she is the largest and best preserved T-rex ever discovered. Although she was discovered in South Dakota, Sue now resides in Chicago, Illinois, at The Field Museum, she is on display for the public to see. Visitors can see up close Sue's features: ribs, forelimbs, and mouth bones, CT scan of her skull the braincase as well as; many other parts. Sue is quite special she is the most complete T-rex fossil ever discovered. While we have a lot to learn about our past from Sue, we may also learn about our present and future Sue has given us much to explore.

Try It
Write four complete sentences each with two independent clauses joined by a semicolon.

_____

_____

_____

_____

_____

_____

_____

Lesson 2.19 Hyphens

Hyphens are used to divide and to create new words.

Use a hyphen to divide the word between lines. Divide words between syllables.
    sanctu-ary   *de-posit*

Do not divide a one syllable word or words with fewer than six letters.
    ball, toy, cedar, book

Divide syllables after vowels if a vowel is a syllable by itself.
    cele-brate   not: *cel-ebrate*

Do not divide one letter from the rest of the word.
    ele-phant   not: *e-lephant*

Hyphens can be used to create new words when combined with *self, ex,* or *great.*
    My *great-grandfather* worked on the railroad.

Solve It

Solve the following puzzle. Place the words from the box in the appropriate spaces. The words must be divided correctly in order to fit into the boxes.

basket	compose	dinosaur	graduate	puppy
bicycle	crocodile	embankment	personal	television

1. __ __ __ __ - __ __ __ __ __ __

2. __ __ __ - __ __ __

3. __ __ __ - __ __ __ __ __ __

4. __ __ __ __ __ - __ __ __ __ __

5. __ __ __ __ __ __ - __ __ __

6. __ __ __ - __ __ __ __

7. __ __ __ __ __ - __ __ __ __

8. __ __ __ __ - __ __ __

9. __ __ __ __ __

10. __ __ __ __ - __ __ __ __

Lesson 2.19 Hyphens

Proof It
The words in this advertisement are broken in the
wrong places. Use the proofreading marks to correct
the placement of the hyphens.

	– deletes letters, words, punctuation
^	– inserts letters, words, punctuation
⌣	– moves punctuation from one place to another

Come and see what's wild in Alaska. Anchorage, A-

laska, in South central Alaska, is home to a wide variety of wildlife.

Anchorage is one of the best cities in the world to view nat-

ure and wildlife at its best. All year long, you are able to see wildlife:

moose, caribou, bears, dall sheep, wolves, whales, ly-

nx, and otters. At the Alaska Wildlife Conservation Center, you can see

wildlife in a special environment. The Alaska Wildlife Conserv-

ation Center is a non-profit organization that serves as a refuge for

orphaned, injured, and ill animals. The center also educates vis-

itors about Alaskan wildlife. The Tony Knowles Trail; a biking, hiking,

and ski trail that runs through Anchorage, is also an excellent viewing spot

for wildlife. Just be careful, we are invading their homes. Treat all an-

imals you see with respect, and with distance. Come and take a walk

on our wild side. Visit Anchorage, Alaska!

Try It
How many *self's, ex's,* and *great's* can you think of? Write at least two of each that
start with these prefixes and a hyphen. Use a dictionary if you need help.

1. _____

2. _____

3. _____

4. _____

5. _____

6. _____

7. _____

8. _____

9. _____

10. _____

11. _____

12. _____

Lesson 2.20 Parentheses

Parentheses are used to show extra material, to set off phrases in a stronger way than commas, and to enclose numbers.

Supplementary, or extra, **material** is a word or phrase that gives additional information.
Those apples *(the ones in the basket)* are good for baking in cobblers.

Sometimes, words or phrases that might be set off with commas are set off with parentheses, instead. It gives the information more emphasis for a stronger phrase.
The television program, *the one that was canceled,* was my favorite.
The television program *(the one that was canceled)* was my favorite.

Parentheses are also used to enclose numbers in a series.
I do not want to go to the movie because *(1)* it is too late, *(2)* it is all the way across town, and *(3)* it is too scary.

Complete It

Complete the following sentences by adding parenthetical phrases from the box to the sentences. Add the parentheses where they belong. The first one is done for you.

(1) (2) (3) with four doors	(1) (2) (3) my best friend	my great-great-grandmother see key

1. The road on this map looks like a two-lane road.

   The road on this map (see key) looks like a two-lane road.

2. The recipe is the best!

   _____

3. Andy is moving to another state.

   _____

4. I love to exercise because it is good for my heart, it gives me energy, and I feel good afterward.

   _____

   _____

5. The new, blue car is the one I want.

   _____

6. Pigs are my favorite animal because they are intelligent, cute, and make "oinking" sounds.

   _____

   _____

Lesson 2.20 Parentheses

Rewrite It
Rewrite the following paragraph. Add parentheses as needed.

     The Japanese Tea Ceremony is an ancient and beautiful ritual. The ceremony is 1 a way of preparing tea, 2 a way of serving tea, and 3 a way of drinking tea. The room where the tea ceremony is held is the teahouse called *chashitsu*. One particular tea ceremony *Chaji* is held to honor guests into a home. The guests 1 enter the tea house from the garden called *roji*, 2 are served a light meal, 3 take a short break in the garden, 4 return to the tea house. At this time, the host 1 prepares a thick tea called koicha, and 2 prepares a thin tea. Lafcadio Hearn an author of books about Japan and Japanese fairy tales said, "The tea ceremony requires years of training and practice... yet the whole of this art, as to its detail, signifies no more than the making and serving of a cup of tea."

_____
_____
_____
_____
_____
_____
_____
_____
_____
_____
_____

Try It
Write one sentence that has supplemental material in parentheses, one sentence that sets off information with emphasis, and one sentence that has numbers and parentheses.

1. _____
2. _____
3. _____

Review Chapter 2 Lessons 8–20

Review: Periods: After Declarative and Imperative Sentences, In Dialogue, In Abbreviations, In Initials, Titles Before Names, Question Marks, Exclamation Points

Putting It Together
The following sentences are missing punctuation. Add periods, question marks, and exclamation points where needed.

1. Don't forget to stop by the store and pick up bread on your way home from school

2. What time is Gillian stopping over

3. Helen said, "The flowers in my garden are beautiful"

4. Look out

5. J R R Tolkien is my favorite author.

6. My dentist is Dr Guten.

7. Do I have an appointment with Dr. Guten on Tuesday

8. Ellen Hobbs, MA is speaking at our school on Friday.

Review: Commas: Series, Direct Address, Multiple Adjectives, Combining Sentences, Set-Off Dialogue, Personal Letters

Proofread the following letter. Add commas where necessary using proofreading mark.

⌃ – inserts commas

6919 Muirfield Rd.
Bloomfield MI 30000
September 23 2008

Dear Carl

I wanted to write you and tell you about my weekend. I went to the Ryder Cup and I saw my favorite players! The Ryder Cup is a golf match between the United States and Europe. It is the only team golf match with a real history. I got to see Tiger Woods Sergio Garcia and Jay Haas. Although you can't say anything during the course of play I yelled out "Tiger you're the best!" between holes. It was great. I bought you a hat at the gift shop and I'll give it to you when I see you winter break. I hope you are well.

Your friend
Mindy

Review Chapter 2 Lessons 8–20

Review: Quotation Marks, Apostrophes, Colons, Semicolons, Hyphens, Parentheses

Rewrite each sentence. Add punctuation where necessary.

1. My great grandmother played softball in college, said Aidan.

_____

_____

2. The doctor said "You'll be fine!"

_____

_____

3. I want to take Ms. Roses class because I she teaches a lot of geography, 2 she takes her classes on field trips, and 3 she is nice.

_____

_____

4. "Charlotte, did our teacher say, the bus for the museum leaves at 9 00?"

_____

_____

5. I am excited about going to the museum of art I want to be an artist someday.

_____

_____

6. Susan got what she had been hoping for a new job.

_____

_____

7. I didnt read the series, <u>The Lord of the Rings</u>, but I loved the movies.

_____

_____

Chapter 3

Lesson 3.1 Irregular Verbs: *Come, Do, Go*

The **present tense** of a verb tells that the action is taking place now or continuously.
> Ted and Parker *come* over every day after school.
> I *do* the crossword puzzles on Sunday.
> Can I *go* with you to the library now?

The **past tense** of a verb tells that the action took place in the past.
> Cassie *came* with us to the movies last weekend.
> I not only *did* the crossword puzzle last Sunday, I *did* the word search, too.
> Renee and Kristen *went* on an archeological dig last semester.

The **past participle** of a verb tells that the action began in the past and was completed in the past. In order to form the past participle, the verb must be preceded by one of the following verbs: *was, were, has, had,* or *have.*
> Karen, Lori, and Blair *had come* with us on our vacation three years in a row.
> The chef checked to see if the cake *was done.*
> Adam *had gone* to see that same movie many times.

Solve It

Find all of the forms of *come, do,* and *go* in the puzzle. The verbs that go with the past participles are also included. The words can be horizontal, vertical, diagonal, backward, and forward.

come	did	went	has
came	done	gone	is
do	go	had	was

```
p  h  m  s  d  e  g  p  o
r  c  o  m  e  m  i  f  k
g  u  g  n  c  w  s  j  s
i  d  h  k  h  a  d  i  y
f  i  o  a  i  s  n  h  l
t  d  s  c  t  s  g  a  m
o  c  o  n  a  o  o  n  c
c  t  e  e  r  m  n  b  g
g  w  a  d  o  n  e  w  x
w  k  d  a  n  h  f  q  t
```

Lesson 3.1 Irregular Verbs: *Come, Do, Go*

Complete It
Complete the following sentences by circling the correct verb in parentheses.

1. Timmy (come, has come) over for dinner every night this week.

2. I can (did, do) my homework now.

3. The class (go, had gone) to the same exhibit last year.

4. Please (came, come) and pick up your order.

5. Andrea (do, has done) that assignment many times before.

6. The butterflies (had come, has come) back to this same location for many years.

7. Lynne and Nicole (gone, went) to see the butterflies at the butterfly house.

8. Meg (did, was done) with her chores before the programs started.

9. Ollie (came, come) home from his vacation with many pictures.

10. Beth and Eddie (go, gone) to the same vet as Eric and Shane.

Try It
Practice writing the present, past, and past participle forms of the verbs *come*, *do*, and *go*. Write one sentence of each type for each verb.

_____

_____

_____

_____

_____

_____

_____

_____

_____

_____

_____

_____

Lesson 3.2 Irregular Verbs: *Run, See, Sit*

The **present tense** of a verb tells that the action is taking place now or continuously.
> Bob and Nelly *run* every day at lunch.
> I *see* the stars and even some planets with this telescope.
> Come and *sit* beside me for dinner.

The **past tense** of a verb tells that the action took place in the past.
> Mike and Jim *ran* together on the high school track team.
> Erica and Karen *saw* the play from first row seats.
> The kitten *sat* on the chair closest to the window.

The **past participle** of a verb tells that the action began in the past and was completed in the past. In order to form the past participle, the verb must be preceded by one of the following verbs: *was, were, has, had,* or *have.*
> The coach *has run* the track many times himself.
> John realized after he sat down that he already *had seen* the film.
> Mr. Chat couldn't believe he *had sat* on his hat.

Match It

Draw a line to match the verbs in Column A with its part of speech in Column B.

Column A	Column B
1. has run	present
2. saw	past
3. sit	past participle

Column A	Column B
4. sat	present
5. was seen	past
6. run	past participle

Lesson 3.2 Irregular Verbs: *Run, See, Sit*

Proof It
Proofread the following paragraph. Use the proofreading marks to correct errors with the use of the verbs *run, see,* and *sit*. Use clues from the rest of the sentence as to what the tense of the sentence should be.

_e_ – deletes letters, words, punctuation
∧ – inserts letters, words, punctuation

They have ran, follow, sniff, have seen, and sometimes they sat. They are an important member of many teams. Who are they? They are rescue dogs. Rescue dogs are important to police departments, fire departments, and many rescue organizations. Rescue dogs can saw and smell things human beings can't. Human rescuers saw these dogs had run through wildernesses looking for missing persons, sniffing for clues along the way. Some dogs ran up snowy mountains to find fallen hikers and skiers. Sometimes they have sat for hours waiting for their turn to seek and rescue. And when they are called, they are ready to go.

Rescue dogs and their guardians are well trained teams. They work together, ran together, play together, and rescue together. These teams go through many hours of intensive training and see and experienced many types of challenging situations. We owe a lot to these hard-working dogs and those who train and love them.

Many believe that rescue dogs run with their noses to the ground in order to pick up scents. It's not necessarily true; rescue dogs can be trained to receive scents from the air and can ran with noses up!

Try It
Practice writing the present, past, and past participle forms of the verbs *run, see,* and *sit*. Write one sentence of each type for each verb.

_____

_____

Lesson 3.3 Adjectives: *Cute, Big, Light*

Adjectives modify, or describe, nouns. **Comparative adjectives** compare two nouns, and **superlative adjectives** compare three or more nouns.

cute/cuter/cutest   big/bigger/biggest   light/lighter/lightest

<u>Describing one noun:</u>

Phoebe has a *cute* puppy.
Melissa has a *big* dog.
That truck carries *light* cargo.

<u>Comparing two nouns:</u>

My pink sweater is *cuter* than my yellow one.
Joe's sandwich is *bigger* than Barney's.
Lance's bicycle is *lighter* than Greg's.

<u>Comparing three or more nouns:</u>

Those are the *cutest* puppets I've ever seen.
The house on the corner has the *biggest* snowman.
My windbreaker is the *lightest* jacket in my closet.

Complete It

Complete the following sentences by circling the correct word or words in parentheses.

1. Of the three bats, Henry's is the (light, lightest).

2. Christina has a very (cute, cuter) kitten.

3. My notebook is (bigger, biggest) than yours.

4. (Light, Lightest) rain fell on the roof.

5. Every mother thinks her child is the (cute, cutest) in the class.

6. After playing soccer, Aaron has a (big, bigger) appetite.

7. I think the cartoon at 8:30 is (cuter, cutest) than the cartoon at 8:00.

8. Jordan's bookbag is (lighter, lightest) than Riley's.

9. Gillian wants to ride on the (big, bigger) roller coaster in the park.

10. Aubrey drew her parents a (cute, cuter) picture.

11. Adam has a (bigger, biggest) lead in the race than Lewis.

12. Of all the boxes, Joe picked the (lighter, lightest) to carry.

Lesson 3.3 Adjectives: *Cute, Big, Light*

Proof It
Proof the body of the following letter, replacing the incorrect form of the adjectives.

> *e* – deletes letters, words, punctuation
> ^ – inserts letters, words, punctuation

Dear Margie,

Today was the best day of my trip to England. I saw the cute show of all. It was a marionette show. Marionettes are cuter, puppet-like figures. They are lightest and small and operated by strings. Stages for performances by people are biggest than for marionette shows, so I sat up close. I learned that puppet theatres have been popular for centuries in Europe, Asia, and America. It was the big form of entertainment for Europeans in the Middle Ages. I think the little children marionettes are cuter, but the animal marionettes are the cute of all. Let's see a show together when I get home!

Your friend,

Barbie

Try It
Write a paragraph describing a performance you have seen. Use at least six adjectives from this lesson.

_____

_____

_____

_____

_____

_____

_____

_____

Lesson 3.4 Adjectives: *More/Most;*
Good/Better/Best; Bad/Worse/Worst

The word *more* before an adjective means it is **comparative**, comparing two nouns. The word *most* before an adjective means it is **superlative**, comparing three or more nouns. The words *more* and *most* are usually used instead of **er** and **est** with adjectives that have more than two syllables.

> Students in the morning class are *more energetic* than students in the afternoon class.
> Please sign the three yellow forms first; they are *most important.*

If you don't know whether to use **er/est** or *more/most,* then say the words out loud. Use the form that sounds best.

Two adjectives do not follow either pattern for making comparative and superlative adjectives. The adjectives *good* and *bad* have their own rules.

> This is *good* strawberry ice cream.
> The strawberry ice cream is *better* than the chocolate ice cream.
> The strawberry ice cream is the *best* ice cream of all.

> That was a *bad* movie.
> The movie was *worse* than the one we saw last week.
> The movie we saw two weeks ago was the *worst* movie of all.

Identify It

Identify each of the following sentences as either a comparative sentence or a superlative sentence. Write **C** for comparative and **S** for superlative. Then, underline the adjectives (including the words *more* or *most*) in the sentences.

1. _____ The most challenging sports competition in the world is the Tour de France.

2. _____ The Tour de France can be ridden in some of the worst weather conditions.

3. _____ One of the best shirts to earn in the Tour de France is the polka-dot jersey.

4. _____ Lance Armstrong is one of the world's most famous bicyclers.

5. _____ Lance Armstrong now has had more specialized training than he did years ago.

6. _____ He is now a better rider than he was years ago.

Lesson 3.4 Adjectives: *More/Most;*
Good/Better/Best; Bad/Worse/Worst

Solve It

The following sentences are not finished. Use the pictures to help you solve the sentences. Write *more, most, good, better, best, bad, worse,* or *worst* in the blanks to solve each sentence. Each word will be used once.

1. I like my ice cream cone _____ than your ice cream cone.

2. This is the _____ banana in the bunch.

3. That was a _____ book.

4. Paula has _____ pencils than Paul.

5. Alice has a _____ cold.

Try It

Write your own sentence for each of the following adjectives: *good, better, best, bad, worse,* and *worst.*

_____

_____

_____

_____

_____

Lesson 3.5 Adjectives and Adverbs: *Bad/Badly, Good/Well, Very* and *Really*

Adverbs modify verbs, adjectives, and other adverbs. Some adverbs are easily confused with adjectives.

Bad is an adjective and *badly* is an adverb. Determine what you are modifying before using *bad* and *badly*.

A *bad* storm is heading our way.

Bad is used as an adjective modifying the noun *storm*. No **ly** is added.

Cami sings *badly*.

Badly is used as an adverb modifying the verb *sings*. Use the **ly** form of bad.

Good is an adjective and *well* is an adverb. Determine what you are modifying before using *good* and *well*.

Claudia is a *good* cook and bakes *well*, too.

In this sentence, the adverb *well* modifies the verb *bakes*. The adjective *good* modifies the noun *cook*.

The words *very* and *really* are both adverbs.

Please talk *very* softly in the library.

The adverb *very* modifies the adverb *softly* that modifies the verb *talk*.

Complete It

Complete the following sentences by circling the correct adverb in parentheses. Underline the verb, adjective, or adverb that it modifies. Then, write what type of word it modifies: **V** for verb, **ADJ** for adjective, **ADV** for adverb, and **N** for noun.

1. _____ Jim was sick and so ran (bad, badly) during the race.

2. _____ Amy had a great day and ran (good, well) in her race.

3. _____ The day I lost the race was a (bad, badly) day for me.

4. _____ I was a (bad, badly) beaten runner.

5. _____ But it was a (good, well) day for my friend.

6. _____ She accepted her praises (good, well).

7. _____ I will train harder so I do (good, well) in my next race.

8. _____ That will be a (good, well) day for the whole team.

Lesson 3.5 Adjectives and Adverbs: *Bad/Badly, Good/Well, Very* and *Really*

Proof It
Proofread the following article using proofreading marks. Look for errors with adjectives and adverbs. When you come to the adverbs *really* or *very*, underline the words they modify.

> *℮* - deletes letters, words, punctuation
> ^ - inserts letters, words, punctuation

Where do you go to find the very best in wildlife viewing? The answer varies greatly. Well viewing can be found all over the United States. One particular wildlife refuge is good hidden. The Arctic National Wildlife Refuge is located in northern Alaska on the Bering Strait. You can only reach it by bush plane. But the travel is worth it with well sightings of caribou, wolves, grizzly and black bears, musk oxen, polar bears, and wolverines. The area is known for badly storms. Visit with a good trained guide.

If it is aquatic animals you really want to see, you should go to the Everglades in Florida. If you paddle good and are in well shape, you can canoe or kayak on the water trails. Visit in January or February, or you may be bad bitten by mosquitoes. Those who visit are really excited to see alligators, dolphins, crocodiles, flamingos, and manatees. From Alaska to Florida and many places in between, well wildlife viewing is there for you to see.

Try It
Write an article describing a school event in which some things went well, and some things didn't go so well. Use each of the words *bad, badly, good, well, really,* and *very* at least once.

_____

_____

_____

_____

_____

_____

_____

Lesson 3.6 Homophones: *Allowed/Aloud, Buy/By, Main/Mane*

Homophones are words that sound the same but have different spellings and different meanings. There are hundreds of homophones in the English language.

allowed: to be permitted   *aloud*: to be audible

buy: to purchase   *by*: to be near

main: the most important   *mane*: hair

If you are unsure about which homophone to use, look up the meanings in a dictionary.

Match It

Read the following sentences. Circle the letter of the definition of the underlined homophone that fits the sentence.

1. Taylor will have many books to <u>buy</u> when he starts college.
   a. to purchase
   b. to be near

2. The horse's <u>mane</u> glistened in the morning sunshine.
   a. the most important
   b. hair

3. My father said we weren't <u>allowed</u> to see that movie.
   a. to be permitted
   b. to be audible

4. Ellen lives <u>by</u> the pond with the ducks and geese.
   a. to purchase
   b. to be near

5. Please underline the sentence with the <u>main</u> idea in this paragraph.
   a. the most important
   b. hair

6. The students will recite the poems <u>aloud</u>.
   a. to be permitted
   b. to be audible

Lesson 3.6 Homophones: *Allowed/Aloud, Buy/By, Main/Mane*

Proof It
Proofread the story, and use proofreading marks to correct the homophones.

- deletes letters, words, punctuation
- inserts letters, words, punctuation

More than anything, Luke wanted a horse for his birthday. He and his family lived on a farm, so why couldn't he have a horse to call his own? So far, he hadn't been aloud to have his own horse. This year was going to be different. Luke's father said he could have a horse if he could by it himself. He would pay Luke for chores he did on the farm. Then, Luke could by the horse he wanted. For his birthday, Luke's parents would by all of the mane supplies and equipment he would need. Luke liked this deal. Then, the horse would really belong to him. It would be his responsibility to feed, clean, and exercise his horse. Luke found the perfect horse at a stable buy their farm. He had beautiful brown hair and a shiny main. Luke was so excited he shouted allowed, "Thank you for my wonderful present! He'll be my friend forever!" Luke was glad he wasn't aloud to have a horse until now. He was more grown up now and could take good care of a horse himself. His horse whinnied allowed. Luke smiled. It was a perfect birthday.

Try It
Write a sentence of your own for each of the six homophones from this lesson: *allowed, aloud, buy, by, main,* and *mane.*

_____

_____

_____

_____

_____

Lesson 3.7 Homophones: *Passed/past, Threw/Through, To/Too*

Homophones are words that sound the same but have different spellings and different meanings. The homophones *passed* and *past*, *threw* and *through*, and *to* and *too* are often confused.

passed: went by	*past*: former
threw: tossed	*through*: finished
to: toward	*too*: also

Complete It

Complete the following sentences by circling the correct homophone in parentheses.

1. Today's lesson is about more than Presidents; it's about their pets, (to, too).

2. President Benjamin Harrison's grandchildren liked to hitch a small cart (to, too) the President's pet goat, His Whiskers, and ride around the White House lawn.

3. Once, His Whiskers escaped (threw, through) an open gate.

4. The President ran after His Whiskers and led the goat and the children back (to, too) the White House.

5. President Lyndon B. Johnson was kind (to, too) a stray when his daughter Luci found a small mutt.

6. President Calvin Coolidge's raccoon, Rebecca, had her own house on White House grounds. He walked (to, too) her house every day and took her on a walk on a leash.

7. Not only did Luci Johnson adopt a stray, but Chelsea Clinton, daughter of President Bill Clinton, did, (to, too).

8. When Chelsea went (to, too) college, the president's secretary, Betty Currie, took in Socks the cat.

9. The pets of (passed, past) Presidents are quite popular with the public.

10. The pets are so popular that a museum, the Presidential Pet Museum near Washington D.C., is dedicated just (to, too) them.

Lesson 3.7 Homophones: *Passed/past, Threw/Through, To/Too*

Find It

Use a dictionary to look up the following groups of homophones. Write their definitions on the lines provided.

1. ad: _____
   add: _____

2. bail: _____
   bale: _____

3. board: _____
   bored: _____

4. bough: _____
   bow: _____

5. capital: _____
   capitol: _____

6. do: _____
   dew: _____
   due: _____

7. fair: _____
   fare: _____

8. feat: _____
   feet: _____

9. flew: _____
   flu: _____
   flue: _____

10. knight: _____
    night: _____

Try It

Choose six of the groups above. Write sentences for all twelve words.

_____

_____

_____

_____

_____

_____

_____

_____

_____

_____

_____

Lesson 3.8 Contractions

An apostrophe is used to substitute letters in **contractions**.

To form a contraction with *am*, drop the **a** and add an apostrophe.
    I am tired today.   *I'm* tired today.

To form a contraction with *are*, drop the **a** and add an apostrophe.
    They are going to the beach.   *They're* going to the beach.

To form a contraction with *is* or *has*, add an apostrophe and keep only the **s**.
    She is ready to go.   *She's* ready to go.
    What has John been doing?   *What's* John been doing?

To form a contraction with *would* or *had*, add an apostrophe and keep only the **d**.
    He would be able to do that.   *He'd* be able to do that.
    I had thought of that.   *I'd* thought of that.

To form a contraction with *will*, drop the **wi** and add an apostrophe where the **wi** was.
    We will get the work done tomorrow.   *We'll* get the work done tomorrow.

To form a contraction with *not*, drop the **o** and add an apostrophe where the **o** was.
    We *should not* go there right now.   We *shouldn't* go there right now.

The contraction for *let us* is *let's*.
    Let us go home.   *Let's* go home.

Match It

Draw a line from Column A to the contraction that could be substituted in Column B.

Column A	Column B
1. I am going to the humane society to adopt a dog.	can't
2. The humane society has many animals up for adoption; it is a great way to save animals.	I'm
3. These animals are strays, or they have been abandoned or turned in as unwanted.	it's
4. They had many pure bred dogs last week.	let's
5. The shelter workers work hard with the animals so they will be ready to go to a good home.	they'd
6. We are also going to look at the cats, rabbits, and ferrets; they all need homes.	they'll
7. I can not wait until I'm 16 and can volunteer to walk dogs.	they've
8. Let us hurry! Our dog is waiting!	we're

Lesson 3.8 Contractions

Solve It
Add the apostrophe where it is needed in each word. Then, write the words the contractions stand for.

1. hes _____

2. youre _____

3. werent _____

4. shouldve _____

5. Im _____

6. shed _____

7. well _____

8. lets _____

9. cant _____

10. youll _____

11. mightve _____

12. heres _____

Try It
Write a sentence for each of the 12 contractions above.

_____

_____

_____

_____

_____

_____

_____

_____

_____

_____

_____

_____

Lesson 3.9 Negatives and Double Negatives

A **negative** sentence states the opposite. Negative words include: *not, no, never, nobody, nowhere, nothing, barely, hardly, scarcely,* and contractions containing the word *not.*

Double negatives occur when two negative words are used in the same sentence. Don't use double negatives; it will make your sentence positive again, and it is poor grammar.

<u>Negative:</u> We do *not* have any soup in the pantry.
<u>Double negative:</u> We do *not* have *no* soup in the pantry.

<u>Negative:</u> I have *nothing* to wear to the party this weekend.
<u>Double negative:</u> I *don't* have *nothing* to wear to the party this weekend.

<u>Negative:</u> Greg can *hardly* put weight on his leg since his knee operation.
<u>Double negative:</u> Greg *can't hardly* put weight on his leg since his knee operation.

Identify It

Identify which of the following sentences have double negatives by writing an **X** on the lines. Then, go back and correct the double negatives by crossing out one of the negatives or by changing the wording.

1. _____ The chef hardly uses any fat in his cooking.

2. _____ I don't like no green peppers on my pizza.

3. _____ I can barely see nothing in this fog.

4. _____ The instructions never say to use a hammer.

5. _____ Nobody hardly showed up at the premier.

6. _____ Nowhere does it say to not add butter.

7. _____ Please do not assign no more homework.

8. _____ We can scarcely finish the work we have now.

9. _____ They don't have no money left for the ride home.

10. _____ I want to go swimming on vacation, but not snorkeling.

11. _____ He can't have no more cookies.

12. _____ I don't want to go nowhere until I've finished my work.

13. _____ She barely can find nothing without her glasses.

14. _____ He can't never lift something that big.

15. _____ We won't plant these flowers until spring.

Lesson 3.9 Negatives and Double Negatives

Rewrite It

As you rewrite the paragraph, correct the double negatives.

Firefighting is a brave and courageous job. If you can't imagine yourself not working hard, then this job isn't for you. Firefighters go through special training. They don't never take training lightly. Some trainees don't make it through this training. Firefighters must train in actual fires. They may find they don't like climbing no ladders that are so high. Some may find they aren't scarcely strong enough. The firefighters who graduate are ready for the job. They don't know nothing about what lies ahead, but they are trained and ready. Firefighters keep us, our pets, and our homes safe. Firefighting is a brave and courageous career to explore.

_____

_____

_____

_____

_____

_____

_____

_____

_____

_____

_____

_____

_____

_____

Try It

Write four negative sentences using each of the following words: *not, nobody, nowhere,* and *nothing.* Do not use double negatives.

_____

_____

_____

_____

Review Chapter 3 Lessons 1–9

Review: Verbs: *Come, Do, Go, Run, See, Sit*

Putting It Together

Complete the following sentences by circling the correct verb tense in parentheses.

1. My mom and dad (came, come) to visit my school for every open house.

2. Members of the track team (ran, run) home from school instead of walking.

3. Mitch (did, do) his homework before he ate dinner.

4. Lori and Darrin (saw, see) last year's parade, but didn't make it this year.

5. They (go, have gone) to the festival since they were children.

6. The birds (sit, have sat) in their nest since early morning.

7. I (do, had done) my chores when I first get home from school.

8. I can (saw, see) much better with my glasses than without.

9. Noah (go, went) with his mother to the store yesterday afternoon.

10. Last evening, I (ran, run) three laps around the track before going home.

11. The rain (come, had come) in downpours throughout the night.

12. They (see, had seen) the nurse long before the doctor arrived.

13. LeeAnn and Robby like to (go, went) to the hockey games every weekend.

14. Mr. Baldwin (run, had run) the lawn mower many times before it quit working.

15. After she had left, the babysitter (came, had come) back to pick up her bookbag.

16. Rosemary wanted Jeanine to (sat, sit) with her.

17. Mr, Walsh (do, has done) that kind of work for years.

18. Bill (sat, sit) and waited patiently for the interview to start.

19. Thomas cannot get his dog to (run, ran).

20. Do you remember the last time we (do, did) this hike?

21. Did you (saw, see) the Wimbledon matches on TV last weekend?

22. Syd (go, went) on a river rafting trip last year.

23. Barbara liked to (ran, run) and swim for exercise.

24. The cook yelled, "(Come, Came) and get it!"

25. Mark (saw, see) three raccoons in his backyard.

Review Chapter 3 Lessons 1–9

Review: Adjectives: *Big/Bigger/Biggest, Light/Lighter/Lightest, More/Most, Good/Better/Best, Bad/Worse/Worst*; Adjectives and Adverbs: *Bad/Badly, Good/Well, Very* and *Really*

Identify the correct use of adjectives and adverbs by circling the correct answer in parentheses.

1. Stephanie thought "The Wizard of Oz" was the (cute, cutest) play she had seen all year.

2. We have to climb over one (big, biggest) rock in order to pass the test.

3. That is the (bigger, biggest) mountain I've ever seen.

4. Clint makes (more, most) money mowing lawns than Perry does selling lemonade.

5. The ice storm we had last night was (worse, worst) than the one we had last year.

6. Going to the beach for vacation is a (good, better) idea than going to the mountains.

7. The blizzard brought the (more, most) snow I had ever seen.

8. Snow skiing is a (good, best) winter sport.

9. I think swimming in the lake in the winter is a (bad, badly) idea.

10. Lakeside is a (good, well) park for hiking and biking.

Review: Homophones: *Allowed/Aloud, Buy/By, Main/Mane, Passed/Past, Threw/Through, To/Too*; Contractions; Negatives and Double Negatives

Proofread the following sentences. Check for incorrect homophones, missing apostrophes, and double negatives.

ℓ – deletes letters, words, punctuation
^ – inserts letters, words, punctuation

1. Diane was aloud to visit her friends after she finished her homework.

2. Lynn wants to by earrings with the money she earns from shoveling snow.

3. Elise brushes her horse's main every morning and every night.

4. Mr. and Mrs. Jones past the turn they were supposed to make into the school.

5. Andrew through the football the farthest.

6. Amy wanted to go to the game, to.

7. Whats the best way to get there?

8. Theyre going the wrong direction.

Chapter 4

Lesson 4.1 Writer's Guide: Prewriting

The five steps of the writing process are **prewriting**, **drafting**, **revising**, **proofreading**, and **publishing**.

Prewriting, the first stage of the writing process, involves planning and organizing. This is the stage where you get the ideas for your paper and start plotting it out.

When you prewrite, you:

- Think of ideas for your topic that are not too narrow or too broad. Write down your chosen ideas.

- Select your favorite topic, the one you think you can write about the best.

- Write down anything that comes to your mind about your chosen topic. Don't worry about grammar and spelling at this stage. This is called *freewriting*.

- Organize your information the way you might organize it in your paper. Use a graphic organizer. Graphic organizers visually represent the layout and ideas for a written paper. Graphic organizers include spider maps, Venn diagrams, story boards, network trees, and outlines.

- Use your graphic organizer to find out what information you already know and what information you need to learn more about.

Prewriting Example

<u>Assignment:</u> biography of a hero

<u>Topic ideas:</u> Martin Luther King, Jr., Eleanor Roosevelt, Jesse Owens, Cleveland Amory, Lance Armstrong, Rachel Carson

<u>Freewriting of selected topic:</u> Cleveland Amory hero of animals. Author. Founder of the Fund for Animals. Wrote <u>The Cat Who Came for Christmas</u> Read Black Beauty as a child and wanted a ranch for rescued animals. Established Black Beauty Ranch for rescued animals.

<u>Graphic organizer:</u>

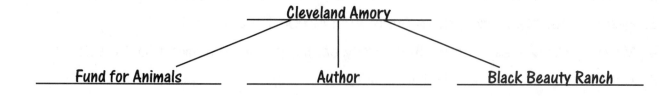

Lesson 4.2 Writer's Guide: Drafting

Drafting involves writing your rough draft. Don't worry too much about grammar and spelling. Write down all of your thoughts about the subject, based on the structure of your graphic organizer.

When you draft, you:

- Write an **introduction** with a topic sentence. Get your readers' attention by stating a startling statistic or asking a question. Explain the purpose of your writing.

- Write the **body** of your paper. Use your graphic organizer to decide how many paragraphs will be included in your paper. Write one paragraph for each idea.

- Write your **conclusion**. Your conclusion will summarize your paper.

Drafting Example

My hero was a hero: a hero to animals. Cleveland Amory (1917-1998) was an author, an animal advocate, and an animal rescuer. Reading Black Beauty as a child inspired a dream for Amory. Cleveland Amory made his dream a reality.

Amory founded The Fund for Animals. The Fund for Animals is an animal advocacy group that campaigns for animal protection. Amory served as its president, without pay, until his death in 1998. Cleveland Amory was an editor. He was an editor for The Saturday Evening Post. He served in World War II. After world war II, he wrote history books that studied society. He was a commentator on The Today Show, a critic for TV guide, a columnist for Saturday Review. Amory especially loved his own cat, Polar Bear, who inspired him to write three instant best-selling books: The Cat Who Came for Christmas, The Cat and the Curmudgeon, and The Best Cat Ever.

When Amory read Black Beauty as a child. When he read Black Beauty, he dreamed of place where animals could roam free and live in caring conditions. The dream is real at Black Beauty Ranch, a sanctuary for abused and abandoned animals The ranch's 1,620 acres serve as home for hundreds of animals, including elephants, horses, burros, ostriches, chimpanzees, and many more. Black Beauty Ranch takes in unwanted, abused, neglected, abandoned, and rescued domestic and exotic animals.

Cleveland Amory is my hero because he is a hero. He worked to make his dreams realities. His best-selling books, the founding of The Fund for Animals, and the opening of Black Beauty Ranch are the legacy of his dreams. Words from Anna Sewell's Black Beauty, the words that inspired Cleveland Amory, are engraved at the entrance to Black Beauty Ranch: "I have nothing to fear; and here my story ends. My troubles are all over, and I am at home." Cleveland Amory died on October 15, 1998. He is buried at Black Beauty Ranch, next to his beloved cat, Polar Bear.

Lesson 4.3 Writer's Guide: Revising

Revising is the time to stop and think about what you have already written. It is time to rewrite.

When you revise, you:

- Add or change words.

- Delete unnecessary words or phrases.

- Move text around.

- Improve the overall flow of your paper.

Revising Example (body of paper)

Cleveland Amory did more than just write about the animals he loved.

Amory founded The Fund for Animals. ^in 1967 The Fund for Animals is ^one of the world's most active an animal advocacy

group that campaigns for animal ^rights and protection. Amory served as its president, without

Amory extended his devotion to animals with Black Beauty Ranch

pay, until his death in 1998. Cleveland Amory ^started his writing career as was an editor. He was an editor for The

^serving in

Saturday Evening Post. He served in World War II. After ^world war II, he wrote history

books that studied society. He was a commentator on The Today Show, a critic for TV

Amory's love of animals, as well as great affection for

guide, a columnist for Saturday Review. ^Amory especially loved his own cat, Polar Bear,

led

who inspired ^him to write three instant best-selling books: The Cat Who Came for

Christmas, The Cat and the Curmudgeon, and The Best Cat Ever.

Cleveland Amory made his childhood dream come true in 1979 when he opened Black Beauty Ranch in Texas.

When Amory read Black Beauty as a child. When he read Black Beauty, ^H he

dreamed of place where animals could roam free and live in caring conditions. The

for hundreds of

dream is real ^at Black Beauty Ranch, a sanctuary for abused and abandoned animals

The ranch's 1,620 acres serve as home for hundreds of animals, including elephants,

animals

horses, burros, ostriches, chimpanzees, and many more. ^Black Beauty Ranch takes in

unwanted, abused, neglected, abandoned, and rescued domestic and exotic

animals.

Lesson 4.4 Writer's Guide: Proofreading

Proofreading is the time to look for more technical errors.

When you proofread, you:

- Check spelling.
- Check grammar.
- Check punctuation.

Proofreading Example (body of paper after revision)

Cleveland Amory started his writing career as an editor for <u>The Saturday Evening Post</u>. After serving in world war II, he wrote history books that studied society. He was a commentator on <u>The Today Show</u>, a critic for <u>TV guide</u>, a columnist for <u>Saturday Review</u>. Amory's love of animals, as well as great affection for his own cat, Polar Bear, led him to three instant best-selling books: <u>The Cat Who Came for Christmas</u>, <u>The Cat and the Curmudgeon</u>, and <u>The Best Cat Ever</u>.

Cleveland Amory did more than just write about the animals he loved. Amory founded The Fund for Animals in 1967. The Fund for Animals is one of the world's most active animal advocacy group that campaigns for animal rights and protection. Amory served as its president, without pay, until his death in 1998. Amory extended his devotion to animals with Black Beauty Ranch.

Cleveland Amory made his childhood dream come true in 1979 when he opened Black Beauty Ranch in Texas. He dreamed of place where animals could roam free and live in caring conditions. The dream is real for hundreds of unwanted, abused, neglected, abandoned, and rescued domestic and exotic animals at Black Beauty Ranch. The ranch's 1,620 acres serve as home for elephants, horses, burros, ostriches, chimpanzees, and many more animals.

Lesson 4.5 Writer's Guide: Publishing

Publishing is the fifth and final stage of the writing process. Write your final copy and decide how you want to publish your work. Here is a list of some ideas:

- Read your paper to family and classmates.

- Illustrate and hang class papers in a "Hall of Fame" in your class or school.

- Publish your work in a school or community newspaper or magazine.

Publishing (compare to the other three versions to see how it has improved)

Biography of a Hero: Cleveland Amory

My hero was a hero: a hero to animals. Cleveland Amory (1917-1998) was an author, an animal advocate, and an animal rescuer. Reading Black Beauty as a child inspired a dream for Amory. Cleveland Amory made his dream a reality.

Cleveland Amory started his writing career as an editor for The Saturday Evening Post. After serving in World War II, Amory wrote history books that studied society. He was a commentator on The Today Show, a critic for TV Guide, and a columnist for Saturday Review. Amory's love of animals, as well as great affection for his own cat Polar Bear, led him to three instant best-selling books: The Cat Who Came for Christmas, The Cat and the Curmudgeon, and The Best Cat Ever.

Cleveland Amory did more than just write about the animals he loved. Amory founded The Fund for Animals in 1967. The Fund for Animals is one of the world's most active animal advocacy groups that campaigns for animal rights and protection. Amory served as its president, without pay, until his death in 1998. Amory extended his devotion to animals with Black Beauty Ranch.

Cleveland Amory made his childhood dream come true in 1979 when he opened Black Beauty Ranch in Texas. He dreamed of a place where animals could roam free and live in caring conditions. The dream is real for hundreds of unwanted, abused, neglected, abandoned, and rescued domestic and exotic animals at Black Beauty Ranch. The ranch's 1,620 acres serve as home for elephants, horses, burros, ostriches, chimpanzees, and many more animals.

Cleveland Amory is my hero because he is a hero. He worked to make his dreams realities. His best-selling books, the founding of The Fund for Animals, and the opening of Black Beauty Ranch are the legacy of his dreams. Words from Anna Sewell's Black Beauty, the words that inspired Cleveland Amory, are engraved at the entrance to Black Beauty Ranch: "I have nothing to fear; and here my story ends. My troubles are all over, and I am at home." Cleveland Amory died on October 15, 1998. He is buried at Black Beauty Ranch, next to his beloved cat, Polar Bear.

Lesson 4.6 Writer's Guide: Evaluating Writing

When you are evaluating your own writing and the writing of others, being a critic is a good thing.

You can learn a lot about how you write by reading and rereading papers you have written. As you continue to write, your techniques will improve. You can look at previous papers and evaluate them. How would you change them to improve them knowing what you know now?

You can also look at the writing of others: classmates, school reporters, newspaper and magazine writers, and authors. Evaluate their writing, too. You can learn about different styles from reading a variety of written works. Be critical with their writing. How would you improve it?

Take the points covered in the Writer's Guide and make a checklist. You can use this checklist to evaluate your writing and others' writing, too. Add other items to the checklist as you come across them or think of them.

Evaluation Checklist

❏ Write an introduction with a topic sentence that will get your readers' attention. Explain the purpose of your writing.

❏ Write the body with one paragraph for each idea.

❏ Write a conclusion that summarizes the paper, stating the main points.

❏ Add or change words.

❏ Delete unnecessary words or phrases.

❏ Move text around.

❏ Improve the overall flow of your paper.

❏ Check spelling.

❏ Check grammar.

❏ Check punctuation.

❏ _____

❏ _____

❏ _____

Lesson 4.7 Writer's Guide: Writing Process Practice

The following pages may be used to practice the writing process.

Prewriting

Assignment: _____

_____

Topic ideas: _____

_____

_____

Freewriting of selected topic: _____

_____

_____

_____

_____

_____

_____

_____

_____

_____

_____

Graphic Organizer:

Lesson 4.7 Writer's Guide: Writing Process Practice

Drafting

_____
_____
_____
_____
_____
_____
_____
_____
_____
_____
_____
_____
_____
_____
_____
_____
_____
_____
_____
_____
_____
_____
_____
_____
_____
_____
_____

Lesson 4.7 Writer's Guide: Writing Process Practice

Revising

Lesson 4.7 Writer's Guide: Writing Process Practice

Proofreading

_____

_____

_____

_____

_____

_____

_____

_____

_____

_____

_____

_____

_____

_____

_____

_____

_____

_____

_____

_____

_____

_____

Lesson 4.7 Writer's Guide: Writing Process Practice

Publishing

Final Draft

_____

_____

_____

_____

_____

_____

_____

_____

_____

_____

_____

_____

_____

_____

_____

_____

_____

_____

_____

_____

_____

_____

_____

_____

_____

_____

_____

_____

_____

_____

_____

_____

Page 6

Articles are specific words that serve as adjectives before a noun. *A*, *an*, and *the* are articles.

The is a **definite article**. It names a specific noun.
   I want to go to *the* park where everyone else went.
   (The article *the* shows that the person wants to go to a specific park.)

A and *an* are **indefinite articles**. They do not name a specific noun.
   I would like to go to *a* park this weekend.
   (The article *a* shows that the person wants to go to any park, and it doesn't matter which one.)

Use *a* when the noun it precedes begins with a consonant or a vowel that sounds like a consonant.
   a dress   a certificate   a book bag   a one-way street

Use *an* when the noun it precedes begins with a vowel or vowel sound.
   an eyebrow   an ostrich   an apple   an honest person

Match It
Match the object in each set with the article that goes with it. Draw a line from Column A to the correct article in Column B. Then, in Column C, write the article and noun together.

Column A	Column B	Column C
nonspecific play	a	a play
specific play	an	the play
nonspecific envelope	the	an envelope

Column A	Column B	Column C
specific beach	a	the beach
nonspecific beach	an	a beach
nonspecific art piece	the	an art

Column A	Column B	Column C
nonspecific hero	a	a hero
nonspecific umbrella	an	an umbrella
specific umbrella	the	the umbrella

Page 7

Match It
Draw a line from Column A to Column B to match nouns. Practice it again by drawing lines from Column C to Column D.

Column A	Column B
person	key
place	police officer
thing	country

Column C	Column D
person	student
place	gate
thing	library

Try It
Write a short paragraph telling about a place you have visited. Use at least six common nouns.

Answers will vary.

Page 8

Proper nouns name specific people, places, and things. In a sentence, the noun is the person, place, or thing that can act or be talked about.

   Dr. Bateman – a specific person
   Dr. Bateman helped our sick puppy.

   Anchorage – a specific place
   Anchorage is a city in Alaska.

   Empire State Building – a specific thing
   The *Empire State Building* is in New York City.

Solve It
Write the correct words from the box to complete Patrick's journal entry. Use only proper nouns.

Uncle Rich	Principal Ron	my principal	planet
my school	tomorrow	The Lord of the Rings	national park
Grand Canyon	Venus	the playground	my uncle
book	Saturday	Highland Park	Pierce School

I love ___Saturday___ mornings. I go to

___Highland Park___ to walk the trails and

read __The Lord of the Rings__. Later, Aunt Pat

and ___Uncle Rich___ come to my house.

We plan our trip to the ___Grand Canyon___.

We use the telescope to look at

___Venus___ when it gets dark. On

Monday, it's back to ___Pierce School___. I

like ___Principal Ron___. He is a good

principal. But I still look forward to the weekend.

Page 9

Find It
Use a dictionary to find at least 10 proper nouns. Remember, proper nouns always begin with a capital letter.

1. _____
2. _____
3. _____
4. _____
5. _____
6. _____
7. _____
8. _____
9. _____
10. _____

Answers will vary and may include words like: Canary Islands, France, Mars, etc.

Try It
Use five proper nouns that you found in the dictionary to write a fictional paragraph. Also include common nouns in your paragraph.

Answers will vary.

A **plural noun** names more than one person, place, or thing. Most nouns are made plural by adding an **s** to the end of the word.

cars   cups   footballs

Some nouns need an **es** added to the end of the word to make them plural. Nouns ending in the letters **s, x,** or **z** or in a **ch** or **sh** sound need **es.**

boss**es**   tax**es**   waltz**es**   bench**es**   dish**es**

If a word ends in the letter **y**, then the **y** is changed to an **i** before adding the **es.**

countr**ies**   cit**ies**   fl**ies**

However, words that end in **y** with a vowel before the **y** only add the **s.**

boys   keys   donkeys

In some cases, the noun has to change its spelling before making the plural form. If a noun ends in **f** or **fe**, and the **f** sound can be heard in the plural form, just add **s**. However, if the final sound of the plural form is **v**, then change the **f** to **ve** and add the **s.**

roofs (**f** sound)   gulfs (**f** sound)
cal**ves** (**v** sound)   loa**ves** (**v** sound)

Identify It
Circle the correct spelling of the plural nouns in the following letter.

Dear Mom and Dad,

Camp is great. I have made a lot of (friendes/(friends)). I have seen many ((animals)/animales). Two little ((foxes)/foxs) ran through the (woodes/(woods)) today. They are pretty. Tomorrow, we are going to hike. But don't worry, we won't go too close to the ((cliffs)/clives) or (valleyes/(valleys)). The ((leaves)/leafs) are falling here and turning color. One leaf is the color of the (cherrys/(cherries)) on our tree at home. I have to go now and help wash the dinner ((dishes)/dishs). After that, I have to practice for one of the (playes/(plays)). I miss you.

Taylor

10

Solve It
Give an example for each of the rules below.

Rule: Nouns ending in the letters **s, x,** or **z** or in a **ch** or **sh** sound need **es**.

Example: <u>Answers will vary</u>.

Rule: Words that end in **y** with a vowel before the **y** add **s**.

Example: <u>Answers will vary</u>.

Rule: If a word ends in the letter **y**, then the **y** is changed to an **i** before adding the **es**.

Example: <u>Answers will vary</u>.

Rule: If a noun ends in **f** or **fe**, and the **f** sound can still be heard in the plural form add **s**.

Example: <u>Answers will vary</u>.

Try It
Make a list of ten of your favorite things. Then, on the lines next to them, write them in their plural form.

singular | plural
1.
2.
3.
4.
5.
6.   Answers will vary.
7.
8.
9.
10.

11

Irregular plural nouns do not have a pattern for changing from singular to plural. These nouns and their plural spellings have to be learned.

Singular noun: | Plural noun:
child | children
man | men
woman | women

Some irregular nouns do not change at all when they are in the plural form. These forms also have to be learned.

Singular noun: | Plural noun:
cod | cod
rye | rye
wheat | wheat

The best way to learn these plural forms is by reading, writing, and practicing. Sometimes, when you read or hear these words used incorrectly, you will be able to tell if they are spelled incorrectly.

Complete It
Read the following paragraph. Choose the correct form of the irregular plural noun in the parentheses and write it on the line. Use a dictionary if you need help.

Hayley and Hannah love animals. They needed to do a project for school that would help their community. They decided to do a project that would teach other (children,childs) _____children_____ about animals. They visited a wildlife center to get information. They learned about (gooses, geese) _____geese_____, (deer, deers) _____deer_____, and (mice, mouses) _____mice_____. They also learned about different (fish, fishes) _____fish_____. They saw (cod, cods) _____cod_____, (trouts, trout) _____trout_____, and (basses, bass) _____bass_____. Hannah liked the (moose, mooses) _____moose_____ the best. Hayley liked the (sheeps, sheep) _____sheep_____. All of the children liked Hayley and Hannah's report and wanted to visit and help the animals, too.

12

Solve It
Find the following irregular plurals in the word search puzzle. The words can be forward, backward, vertical, horizontal, or diagonal.

bass | mice
children | moose
cod | rye
deer | sheep
fish | trout
geese | wheat
men | women

Try It
Choose five singular nouns and write their plural forms. Remember, these are all irregular plural nouns. Use a dictionary if you need help.

singular noun | plural noun
1.
2.
3.   Answers will vary.
4.
5.

13

Answer Key

Page 14

A **pronoun** is a word used in place of a noun. Pronouns can make writing and speaking more interesting. **Subject pronouns** are pronouns that replace the subject of the sentence.

Pancakes are great for breakfast. Pancakes taste good with syrup.
Pancakes are great for breakfast. *They* taste good with syrup.

In the example above, the pronoun *they* is a substitute for the noun *pancakes*.

Singular subject pronouns:
I, you, he, she, it

Plural subject pronouns:
we, you, they

Singular subject nouns:
Debbie likes cats.
Lynn likes to run.
Ed works for a newspaper.
Carol is a teacher.
Bicycling is their favorite sport.

Singular subject pronouns:
I like cats.
You like to run.
He works for a newspaper.
She is a teacher.
It is their favorite sport.

Plural subject nouns:
Greg and Cliff are brothers.
Lisa and Claudia are friends.
Jennifer and Julie are tennis partners.

Plural subject pronouns:
We are brothers.
You are friends.
They are tennis partners.

Match It
Match the following pronouns with the nouns they could replace. Write the correct answer or answers to Column A in Column B. There may be more than one correct answer.

I	he	it	
you	she	we	they

Column A	Column B
Jack and Jennifer	you, we, they
Nicole	I, you, she
ball	it
Josh	I, you, he
cars	they

14

Page 15

Complete It
Choose a subject pronoun to complete the following passage. Each word may be used more than once.

I	he	it		
you	she	we		they

"Chris, are _____you_____ awake?" Mrs. Johnson called from downstairs.

"_____I_____ can't find my shoes. Do _____you_____ know where _____they_____ are?" Chris shouted.

"Ask your sister. Maybe _____she_____ has seen them." answered Mrs. Johnson.

Chris knocked on Kendra's door. "Have _____you_____ seen my shoes? "_____I_____ saw one earlier. _____it_____ was in the dog's mouth," Kendra replied.

"Mom, where's Toby?" Chris scrambled downstairs. "_____I_____ am going to be late for school!"

Mr. Johnson answered. "Toby's out back, and it looks like that little guy is digging a hole. Wait, _____he_____ is definitely covering something up. __We or You__ better get out there!"

Try It
Continue the story above using all of the subject pronouns from the box.

_____

_____

Answers will vary.

_____

_____

15

Page 16

A **pronoun** is a word used in place of a noun. Pronouns can make writing and speaking more interesting. An **object pronoun** replaces the noun that is the receiver of the action in the sentence.

Mrs. Johnson cooked dinner for Mr. Johnson.
Mrs. Johnson cooked dinner for *him*.

In this example, the object pronoun *him* is a substitute for the object noun *Mr. Johnson*.

Singular object pronouns:
me   Mom cooked dinner for me.
you   Mom cooked dinner for you.
him   Mom cooked dinner for him.
her   Mom cooked dinner for her.
it   Mom cooked it.

Plural object pronouns:
us   Mom cooked dinner for us.
you   Mom cooked dinner for you.
them   Mom cooked dinner for them.

Identify It
Circle the errors in object pronoun use in the following school note. Write the correct object pronoun above the mistake. Not all object pronouns used in this note are mistakes.

The fifth-grade class at Riverview Elementary School is taking a field trip to the Science Museum on Wednesday, February 9. Your child has a permission slip. Please sign ⟨her⟩[*me*]. Return it to ⟨you⟩[*her*] by Friday, February 4. Principal Ann will be checking them. I will give them to ⟨it⟩[*me*]. Please fill in your child's name on the nametag and return it to ⟨you⟩. Mr. Baum, the director of the Science Museum, will be checking ⟨it⟩[*them*] I will give ⟨them⟩[*them*] to ⟨me⟩[*him*]. Your child will write a report about their visit. I will read ⟨you⟩. I will also give ⟨him⟩ to you to read. Principal Ann and I will post the reports in the school. Please return them to ⟨them⟩[*us*].

Thank you,

Mrs. Jones

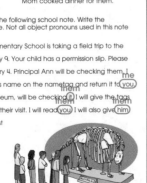

16

Page 17

Rewrite It
Rewrite the following sentences. Replace the underlined object nouns with object pronouns.

1. I needed a pencil. Paul gave his pencil to J.
   I needed a pencil. Paul gave his pencil to me.

2. My cousin and I wanted to go the movies. Dad drove my cousin and J.
   My cousin and I wanted to go the movies. Dad drove us.

3. Tom drew a picture for his big brother, Brian. Tom likes drawing pictures for Brian.
   Tom drew a picture for his big brother, Brian. Tom likes drawing pictures for him.

4. Cathy and Marie won the game. The trophy goes to Cathy and Marie.
   Cathy and Marie won the game. The trophy goes to them.

5. Michelle cooked dinner for her roommate, Jill. Michelle is a good cook and likes to cook for Jill.
   Michelle cooked dinner for her roommate Jill. Michelle is a good cook and likes to cook for her.

6. Michelle cooked spaghetti. She cooked spaghetti with sauce.
   Michelle cooked spaghetti. She cooked it with sauce.

Try It
Write five more sentences that use object pronouns.

1. _____
2. _____
3. _____
4. Answers will vary.
5. _____

17

Answer Key

A **pronoun** replaces a noun in a sentence. The noun that is replaced is called the **antecedent**. All pronouns have antecedents. Pronouns must agree in gender and number with their antecedents and what their antecedents refer to.

> Tony must bring his own lunch to the picnic.
> *He* must bring *his* own lunch to the picnic. (agrees in gender)
> Not: *He* must bring *her* own lunch to the picnic. (does not agree in gender)

> Tony must bring *three* lunches to the picnic.
> Tony must bring *them* to the picnic. (agrees in number)
> Not: Tony must bring *it* to the picnic. (does not agree in number)

Complete It
Circle the correct pronoun in parentheses. Remember that pronouns must agree in both gender and number.

1. Austin did well on (her, his) English report.
2. Austin didn't do well on (his, its) math test.
3. He missed eight problems. (He, They) were hard.
4. Charlotte did well on (her, his) math test.
5. Charlotte didn't do well on (her, them) English report.
6. She made six mistakes in grammar. (They, She) were spelling and punctuation errors.
7. Austin tutored Charlotte with (its, her) grammar skills.
8. Charlotte tutored Austin with (his, her) math skills.
9. Charlotte took Austin to dinner at (her, them) father's restaurant.
10. They ate a small veggie pizza. (Its, It) was delicious.
11. Charlotte and Austin also went to see a movie. (She, They) went to see a comedy.
12. The movie was funny, and (it, they) made them both laugh.

18

Solve It
Solve the following riddle by choosing words from the box to fill in the blanks.

his	it
her	them

Who ate the pizza with pepper?
Who ate the pizza with _____it_____?
Charlotte ate the pizza with pepper.
She ate ____her____ pizza with _____it_____.
Who ordered a salad with tomatoes?
Who ordered a salad with ____them____?
Austin ordered the salad with tomatoes.
He ordered ____his____ salad with ____them____.
I like pizza with _Answers will vary._. (fill in your favorite)
I like pizza with _Answers will vary._. (word from the box)
I like salad with _Answers will vary._. (fill in your favorite)
I like salad with _Answers will vary._. (word from the box)

Try It
Write a letter to your best friend telling about a recent event at school. Include at least four pronouns and antecedents in your letter.

Answers will vary.

19

A **verb** is a word that tells the action or the state of being in a sentence.

> The dogs *sniff* the flowers.

In this sentence, *sniff* is the verb. It tells the action of the sentence. This sentence is in the present tense. The action is taking place now.

> Kevin *talked* about the game last night.

In this sentence, *talked* is the verb. It tells the action of the sentence. This sentence is in the past tense. The action took place in the past. Add **ed** to the present tense of a regular verb to make it past tense. If the word already ends in the letter **e**, just add the letter **d**.

Match It
Match the present tense verb forms in Column A with their past tense form in Column B.

Column A	Column B
add	whispered
ask	asked
call	yelled
dance	added
gasp	gasped
joke	warned
look	called
love	reported
note	danced
order	ordered
observe	noted
report	loved
warn	observed
whisper	looked
yell	joked

20

Complete It
Use the same words from page 20 to complete the following sentences. Choose the correct form, either present or past tense.

1. Quinten ____asked____ a good question in science class earlier.
2. As they look at the picture, the ladies ____gasp____ at its beauty.
3. I ____observe____ at the stars as I walk through the planetarium.
4. Kelly and Taylor, please ____note____ that in your report.
5. Shelly and Dylan ____call____ when they are late.
6. The spectators ____yelled____ and cheered many times during the game last night.
7. Jim fell on the ice. But he ____joked____ about it later.
8. ____Warn____ the passengers, now!
9. May I have some milk? I want to ____add____ it to my coffee.
10. Carl ____ordered____ waffles for breakfast.

Try It
Write a fictional paragraph. Use at least three of the verbs from this lesson. Use their present or past tense forms, or both. Use at least three more verbs (present and/or past) of your own choosing.

Answers will vary.

21

Page 22

Irregular verbs do not follow the same rules as regular verbs when forming their past tense. They must be learned. Below is a list of some of the common irregular verbs in their present and past tense forms.

Present:	Past:
am	was
begin	began
bring	brought
do	did
eat	ate
get	got
is	was
let	let
put	put
rise	rose
sleep	slept
think	thought

Rewrite It

Rewrite each sentence using a different tense. For example, if the sentence is in the present, rewrite it in the past. Remember, if you change the tense of the verb, forms of other words in the sentence may change also. Use a dictionary if you need help.

1. The teacher said to begin the test now.
   We began the test when the teacher gave the signal.

2. The cup broke when I dropped it.
   The cup will break if you drop it.

3. I drive my car to work.
   I drove my car to work yesterday.

4. Michelle and Ray ate all of the pizza.
   Will Michelle and Ray eat all of the pizza?

5. I keep your secret.
   I kept your secret.

6. Let's make a cake for dessert.
   We made a cake for dessert last evening.

Answers will vary.

22

Page 23

Proof It

Proofread the following paragraph. Use the proofreading marks to delete the irregular present and past tense verbs that are used incorrectly. Write the correct word above the incorrect word. Use a dictionary if you need help.

| ℯ - deletes words or letters |
| ^ - inserts words or letters |

Do you ~~know~~ (know) the name of the very first national park? It ~~was~~ (was) Yellowstone National Park. It ~~is~~ (sits) founded in 1872. Yellowstone ~~sits~~ (sits) in three states: Wyoming, Montana, and Idaho. Hot springs cut into the land of Yellowstone. Old Faithful and Mammoth Hot Springs ~~get~~ (get) the most attention from visitors. The spray from Old Faithful can ~~rise~~ (rise) 150 feet into the air. Mammoth Hot Springs continues to ~~grow~~ (grow) to this day. Many animals ~~live~~ (make) in the park. Bears, mountain sheep, elk, bison, moose, and deer, and other wildlife ~~made~~ their home in Yellowstone National Park. Thousands of visitors ~~come~~ (come) to the park every year.

Try It

Choose four present and four past tense irregular verbs from the list on page 22. Write a fictional paragraph using these verbs.

Answers will vary.

23

Page 24

Action verbs tell the action of the sentence. Action verbs come in both regular and irregular forms. They also have present, past, and future tense forms.

Sarah and Nancy *jump* rope at lunch time. (present)
Sarah and Nancy *jumped* rope after school yesterday. (past)
Sarah and Nancy *will jump* rope at lunch and after school tomorrow. (future)

Syd is going to *run* on the track team. (present)
Syd *ran* on the track team last year. (past)
Syd *will run* on the track team next year, too. (future)

Solve It

Complete the crossword puzzle using the words from the box.

| bellowed | crashed | dug | throw |
| bounce | danced | skipped | travel |

Across

3. Alan ____danced____ for hours at the party.

4. The announcement ____bellowed____ across the auditorium.

5. The students ____dug____ for buried fossils.

6. Karen and Marc will ____travel____ to the Caribbean for their vacations.

Down

1. The preschoolers ____skipped____ home from school.

2. The pan ____crashed____ to the floor when my sleeve caught the handle.

4. Which ball do you think will ____bounce____ the highest?

6. ____Throw____ the ball to me!

24

Page 25

Identify It

Circle the action verb in each of the following sentences. Then, replace the verb with another action verb of your own.

1. The hungry travelers (gulped) the snacks.
2. Cami (spun) around and around in her new dress.
3. The papers (fluttered) around the room when the fan started.
4. The puppies (yelped) all night.
5. Kate and Brad (sprung) out of their seats.
6. Many birds (crunched) the seeds in the feeder.
7. The toddlers (screamed) with delight at the clown.
8. The corn kernels (hopped) in the hot oil.
9. The colorful photograph (leapt) off the page in the fashion magazine.
10. Bell's earrings (sparkled) in the sunlight.

Answers will vary.

Try It

Write a paragraph using ten action verbs that you did not use above.

Answers will vary.

25

Helping verbs are not main verbs. Helping verbs help to form some of the tenses of main verbs. Helping verbs express time and mood.

Helping verbs:
shall   may
will   have
could   had
would   has
should   do
must   did
can

She *could run* for miles and miles.

The forms of the verb *to be* are also helping verbs.
is   are   was   were   am   been

An **ing** verb is a clue that there is a helping verb in the sentence.
She *was running* for miles and miles.

Sometimes, more than one helping verb is used in a sentence. This is called a **verb phrase**.
She *had been running* for miles and miles.

Identify It
Circle the letter of the sentence that contains a helping verb. Remember, helping verbs help to set the time and mood of sentences.

1. a. We shall all go to the movies.
   b. We went to the movies.
   c. They ran to the movies.

2. a. Jake helped me with my homework.
   b. Jake will help me with my homework.
   c. Jake helps me with my homework every day.

3. a. I could study all night for the test.
   b. I studied for the test.
   c. I studied with Carol.

4. a. Cheryl only accepted the best.
   b. Cheryl accepted nothing less than perfection.
   c. Cheryl would accept nothing less.

5. a. I should think so!
   b. I think so.
   c. I think you are correct.

26

Complete It
Choose a helping verb or verb phrase from the box to complete each sentence. Then, circle the main verb of the sentence. Sometimes there is a word between the helping and main verbs.

have	is	were
had	are	am
has	was	been

1. We __have__ __been__ (planning) our vacation for many months.
2. I __am or was__ (looking) forward to it.
3. We __are__ (traveling) by ship.
4. We __had__ (to visit) a travel agent last week to get our tickets.
5. It __was or is__ fun (choosing) the ship.

Try It
Write ten sentences using a different helping verb or verb phrase in each.

Answers will vary.

27

Linking verbs are not main verbs. Linking verbs connect, or link, a subject to a noun or adjective. They do not express an action. A verb or adjective will follow these linking verbs in the sentence.

The most common linking verbs are the forms of the verb *be*:
What time *is* it?
We *are* ten minutes away.
What *was* that sound?
There *were* many people in line at the store.
I've *been* sick.
I *am* tired, Dad.

Other linking verbs are those of the five senses:
Do you *smell* that?
You don't *look* too good.
Did the milk *taste* funny?
I don't *feel* too well.
That plan *sounds* good.

Other linking verbs reflect a state of being:
You *appear* ready.
I *seem* better today.
You have *become* very tall.
Tom and Tammy *grow* happier every day.
I will *remain* here tonight.

Identify It
Circle the linking verb and underline the noun or adjective that is linked to the subject.

1. The book is good.
2. The flowers smell sweet.
3. The team appears disorganized.
4. The apples are bad.
5. Sharon looks fantastic tonight.
6. We were late.
7. The pear was tasty.
8. I am cold.

28

Rewrite It
Rewrite each of the sentences with a linking verb from the box. Notice how using other forms of linking verbs add variety to your sentences.

grows	been	sounds
has	remained	tastes

1. The water from the faucet is bad.
   The water from the faucet tastes bad.
2. The older woman in the play is weary.
   The older woman in the play grows weary.
3. The trip is long.
   The trip has been long.
4. Walking, instead of riding, is great.
   Walking, instead of riding, sounds great.
5. The team is disorganized after half time.
   The team remained disorganized after half time.

Try It
Write a paragraph using at least eight of the linking verbs on page 28. Remember, linking verbs link the subject of the sentence to either a noun or an adjective.

Answers will vary.

29

Answer Key

Verbs must agree in number with the subject of the sentence. If the subject is singular, use a singular verb. If the subject is plural, make sure to use a plural verb.

The shirt *fits* just right.   The movies *were* sold out.

If the subject is a **compound subject**, two or more subjects, connected by the word *and*, then a plural verb is needed.

Erika and Chris *photograph* the birds.   Erika *photographs* the birds.

If the subject is a compound subject connected by the words *or* or *nor*, then the verb will agree with the subject that is closer to the verb.

Neither Wanita nor Susan *likes* chocolate pie. (Susan likes)
Does Wanita or her sisters *like* chocolate pie? (sisters like)

If the subject and the verb are separated by a word or words, be sure that the verb still agrees with the subject.

Susan, as well as her coworkers, *wants* to complete the project. (Susan wants)

If the subject is a **collective noun**, a singular word that represents a group, like *family* and *team*, then a singular verb is generally used.

The family *is* ready to go.   The team *runs* one mile every day.

When using the phrases *there is, there are, here is,* and *here are,* make sure that the subjects and verbs agree.

There is one piece of pizza left.   Here is the right path to take.
There are many pieces left.   Here are the bikes we're supposed to use.

Complete It
Circle the correct verb for each sentence.

1. Troy (help, (helps)) his sister with her homework after school.
2. Troy and Billy ((help), helps) their sister with her homework after school.
3. Does Sally or her brothers ((bike), bikes) to school?
4. There ((is), are) one store that I like at that mall.
5. Here (is, (are)) the books on that subject.

30

Proof It
Proofread the following paragraph, correcting the subject-verb agreement mistakes as you go. Use the proofreading key to mark the mistakes and insert the correction.

> ⌐ℓ – deletes words or letters
> ^ – inserts words or letters

Tiger Woods' real first name is Eldrick, and he ~~were~~ was born on December 30, 1975. Fans all over the world saluted him as one of the greatest golfers of all time. He became a professional golfer in 1996. In 2001, Tiger held all four professional major championships at one time, the first golfer ever to do so. He ~~were~~ was also the first golfer of African American or Asian descent to win a major championship. No sportsperson ~~have~~ has ever been awarded Sports Illustrated Sportsman of the Year twice—except Tiger. Tiger and his father started the Tiger Woods Foundation. The foundation support*s* community-based programs that promote health, education, and welfare for children. So, how did Tiger get*s* his nickname? Tiger ~~were~~ was named after a Vietnamese soldier who was a friend of his father. Tiger's father had given the same nickname to his friend.

Try It
Write a paragraph with four sentences about your favorite sport. Be sure that the subjects and verbs agree.

Answers will vary.

31

Adjectives are words used to describe a noun or pronoun. Using colorful, lively, descriptive adjectives makes writing and speaking more interesting.

Most adjectives are **common adjectives** and are not capitalized. They can be found before or after the noun they describe.

It was a *breezy* day.   The day was *breezy*.

The adjective *breezy* tells something about, or describes, the noun *day*.

Proper adjectives are formed from proper nouns and are always capitalized.

The chef likes baking his pizzas in the *Italian* oven.

The proper adjective *Italian* describes what kind of oven it is.

Solve It
Unscramble the words to reveal adjectives that might describe a butterfly.

1. e b f a u t u l i ___beautiful___
2. r o f c l o l u ___colorful___
3. t e r p t y ___pretty___
4. g r h i t b ___bright___

Now write a list of ten adjectives that describe your favorite animals.

Animal: _____

1. _____   6. _____
2. _____   7. _____
3. _____ Answers will vary.
4. _____   9. _____
5. _____   10. _____

32

Rewrite It
Add an adjective that describes each noun in bold. Remember, adjectives can come before or after the noun they describe.

Candice and Danny were 12-year-old twins. They wanted a _____ **pet** for their birthday.

"Do you want a **dog** that is _____ or a **cat** that is _____?" asked their mother.

"You must understand," their mother continued, "pets are a _____ **responsibility**. Are you ready for this ~~resp~~...

Candice and Dann[y]   Answers will vary.   kind to animals, and they were ready for this _____ **job**.

On their birthday, Candice and Danny's _____ **parents** took them to their local animal shelter. There, they found a **dog** that was _____ and a _____ **cat**.

Try It
Write a paragraph about your favorite movie using ten different adjectives.

Answers will vary.

33

Answer Key

Adverbs are words used to describe a verb, an adjective, or another adverb. An adverb tells *how, why, when, where, how often,* and *how much.* Adverbs often end in **ly** (but not always).

How?		**Where?**

John drove *carefully* on the slick road. The weather *outside* was rainy. It seemed

How often?	**When?**	**How?**

like it would *never* stop raining. *Tomorrow, hopefully* the weather will be better.

Identify It
Circle the letter of the sentence that contains an adverb. Remember, adverbs modify verbs, adjectives, and other adverbs.

1. (a.) Lisa quickly finished work so she could go to dinner.
   b. Lisa finished work so she could go to dinner.
   c. Lisa did not finish her work.

2. a. Rachel cooked as if for a feast.
   b. Rachel didn't cook.
   (c.) Rachel cooked the meal today so it would be ready for the feast.

3. a. Fruit makes a delicious dessert.
   (b.) Fruit often makes a delicious dessert.
   c. Fruit is dessert.

4. (a.) The kittens purr very loudly when they are sleeping.
   b. The kittens purr.
   c. The kittens purr when they sleep.

5. a. Birds eat seeds.
   b. Birds eat tiny seeds from a feeder.
   (c.) Birds eat many tiny seeds from the feeder in the winter.

6. (a.) The snow falling outside is beautiful.
   b. The snow is beautiful.
   c. The snowballs are cold and sticky.

7. a. Please ask the clerk if they have more berries.
   (b.) Please politely ask the clerk if they have more berries.
   c. Please ask the clerk if they have more fresh berries.

34

Identify It
Circle the adverbs in the following paragraphs. Then, underline the verb, adjective, or other adverb they describe.

The Emperor's New Clothes, The Snow Queen, and *The Little Mermaid* are just a few fairy tales written by a (remarkably) famous writer. Who so (colorfully) wrote about a little match girl, a brave tin soldier, and an ugly duckling? Hans Christian Andersen did.

Hans Christian Andersen was born (poor) in 1805 in a town in Denmark. What extra money the family had they (eagerly) spent at the theatre. When they didn't have money for tickets, Hans would (quietly) sit (outside) the theatre (actively) reading the playbill. He knew he would (definitely) follow his love of literature and the theatre as a career. With help from grant money, Hans completed school at the University of Copenhagen and became a writer. He wrote (more) than 150 fairy tales. They have been translated into (more) than 100 languages. *The Ugly Duckling,* a tale of self-discovery, was known to be (partly) an autobiography. Hans also wrote plays, poetry, and travelogues. Hans Christian Andersen remains one of the world's (best) known and (most) translated authors.

Try It
Write ten sentences with at least one adverb in each.

1. _____
2. _____
3. _____
4. _____
5. _____
6. _____   Answers will vary.
7. _____
8. _____
9. _____
10. _____

35

Conjunctions are connectors. They connect individual words or groups of words in sentences. There are three kinds of conjunctions.

Coordinate conjunctions connect words, phrases, or clauses, using words like *and, but,* and *or.*
   The snow is cold *and* fluffy.
   Chris likes soccer, *but* Samantha likes football.

Correlative conjunctions are used with pairs and are used together. *Both/and, either/or,* and *neither/nor* are examples of correlative conjunctions.
   Both Tammy *and* Tara went to the play. (*Tammy* and *Tara* are a pair.)

Subordinate conjunctions connect two clauses that are not equal. They connect dependent clauses to independent clauses. *After, as long as, since,* and *while* are examples of subordinate conjunctions.
   They run *after* the sun goes down. (dependent clause: *after the sun goes down*)

Complete It
Complete the following sentences with a conjunction from the box.

and	both/and	neither/nor	as long as
but	either/or	after	since

1. Tabitha wanted to have pretzels for a snack _____ **but** _____ Kisha wanted snowcones.

2. _____ **Neither** _____ red _____ **nor** _____ orange was used in the mural.

3. Taylor wanted to go skiing today _____ **after** _____ the big snowfall.

4. Kari didn't go biking _____ **since** _____ it was storming.

5. _____ **Both** _____ Buster _____ **and** _____ Buzz passed puppy training class.

6. Trevor wanted to stay inside and play board games ___ **as** ___ **long** ___ **as** ___ it was still raining.

7. _____ **Either** _____ take out the trash _____ **or** _____ walk the dog.

8. We were going to see a movie, _____ **but** _____ we went out to eat, instead.

More than one answer may be correct. Possible answers given. Make sure the given answer is from the correct category of either coordinate, correlative, or subordinate.

36

Identify It
Identify the conjunctions in the following sentences as coordinate, correlative, or subordinate. Write **CD** for coordinate, **CR** for correlative, or **S** for subordinate after each sentence.

1. __CD__ Are we going to go biking or hiking on Saturday?

2. __CR__ Neither pasta nor pizza was offered on the menu.

3. __S__ As long as it's raining, we may as well get our homework done.

4. __CR__ Either Rachel or Carrie will be voted president of the class.

5. __S__ Let's walk to school since it is a sunny, warm day.

6. __CD__ Todd wants to play baseball this weekend but he has a class in the morning.

7. __S__ While we are waiting in line, let's get some popcorn.

8. __CR__ Both the girls and the boys' teams are going to the championship.

9. __CD__ Grant wants mushrooms and peppers on his pizza.

10. __S__ After this week, there's only six weeks of school this year.

Try It
Write five sentences of your own using the conjunctions. Use two conjunctions from each category.

1. _____
   _____
2. _____
   _____
3. _____
   Answers will vary.
4. _____
   _____
5. _____
   _____

37

Page 38

An **interjection** is a one- or two-word phrase used to express surprise or strong emotion.

Common interjections:

Ah	Hurray
Aha	Oh
Alas	Ouch
Aw	Uh
Cheers	Uh-huh
Eh	Uh-uh
Hey	Well
Hi	Wow
Huh	Yeah

An exclamation mark is usually used after an interjection to separate it from the rest of the sentence.

Oh! I'm so happy that you can make the trip!

If the feeling isn't quite as strong, a comma is used in place of the exclamation point.

Oh, that's too bad he won't be joining us.

Sometimes question marks are used as an interjection's punctuation.

Eh? Is that really true?

Find It

Use a dictionary to look up each of the following interjections. Write the word's part of speech and the dictionary definition. Then, use each interjection in a sentence.

1. ah - _____

2. alas - _____

3. eh - _____

4. hey - _____

5. oh - _____

6. ouch - _____

Answers will vary depending on the dictionary used.

38

Page 39

Rewrite It

Carl and Dylan are trying to get a game of backyard baseball started. Rewrite the dialogue to include interjections that will make the passage more lively and fun to read.

"Dylan, are you coming?" Carl yelled up to Dylan's open window. He saw Dylan grab his bat. "Everyone's waiting! And don't forget your mitt!"

"What did you say? I can't hear you." Dylan shouted from somewhere in the house. A second later, he opened the front door and jumped off the front porch, skipping the three steps. He did not have his mitt.

"I told you not to forget your mitt!" Carl rolled his eyes. Dylan was always forgetting something.

"I've got it right here," Dylan pulled his mitt out from behind him with a big grin. "I heard you the whole time!"

"You're funny! Now, let's get going! We'll be lucky if we get there by the seventh-inning stretch!"

_____

Answers will vary.

39

Page 40

Prepositions are words or groups of words that show the relationship between a noun or pronoun (the object of the sentence) and another word in the sentence. A prepositional phrase includes the preposition, the object of the preposition, and the modifiers (describes other words) of the object. Prepositional phrases tell about *when* or *where* something is happening.

The students walked **across** the street.
(*across* is the preposition; *street* is the object; *across the street* is the prepositional phrase)

The students walked **alongside** the small park.
(*alongside* is the preposition; *park* is the object; *small* is the modifier; *alongside the small park* is the prepositional phrase)

Common prepositions:

above	behind	for	over
across	below	from	to
after	beneath	in	toward
along	beside	inside	under
around	between	into	until
at	by	near	up
away	down	off	with
because	during	on	within
before	except	outside	without

Identify It

Identify the preposition, object, and modifier in each of the following sentences. Write a **P** above the preposition, an **O** above the object, and an **M** above the modifier.

1. The students played outside at the late recess.
   (P) outside (M) late (O) recess

2. The horse jumped over the high fence.
   (P) over (M) high (O) fence

3. Alice walked out of the scary movie.
   (P) out of (M) scary (O) movie

4. Timmy looked down the deep well.
   (P) down (M) deep (O) well

5. The paper fell underneath the small bookcase.
   (P) underneath (M) small (O) bookcase

40

Page 41

Solve It

Write a preposition that answers the questions below. Use the list of page 40 if you need help.

Prepositions

Where did you put it?   When did you go?   Where did you go?

above _____   after _____   inside _____

Answers will vary.

Try It

Write a journal entry about what you did yesterday. Use at least six prepositions. Once you have written your entry, underline all of the prepositions you used.

_____

Answers will vary.

41

Articles are specific words that serve as adjectives before a noun. *A, an,* and *the* are articles.

The is a **definite article**. It names a specific noun.

I want to go to *the* park where everyone else went.
(The article *the* shows that the person wants to go to a specific park.)

A and *an* are **indefinite articles**. They do not name a specific noun.

I would like to go to *a* park this weekend.
(The article *a* shows that the person wants to go to any park, and it doesn't matter which one.)

Use *a* when the noun it precedes begins with a consonant or a vowel that sounds like a consonant.

a dress   a certificate   a book bag   a one-way street

Use *an* when the noun it precedes begins with a vowel or vowel sound.

an eyebrow   an ostrich   an apple   an honest person

Match It
Match the object in each set with the article that goes with it. Draw an line from Column A to the correct article in Column B. Then, in Column C, write the article and noun together.

Column A	Column B	Column C
nonspecific play	a	a play
specific play	an	the play
nonspecific envelope	the	an envelope

Column A	Column B	Column C
specific beach	a	the beach
nonspecific beach	an	a beach
nonspecific art piece	the	an art

Column A	Column B	Column C
nonspecific hero	a	a hero
nonspecific umbrella	an	an umbrella
specific umbrella	the	the umbrella

42

Proof It
Proofread the following paragraph. Look for mistakes in the use of articles. Use the proof marks to delete incorrect words and insert the correct words.

- deletes words or letters
- inserts words or letters

You've probably read much about the White House, the Washington Memorial, and the Lincoln Memorial in Washington, D.C. But how much do you know about the U.S. Capitol Building? The U.S. Capitol is not just a building in Washington, D.C. It is symbolically and architecturally important. It also has practical significance. The U.S. Capitol is the home of the House of Representatives and the Senate. If visiting Washington, D.C., the dome at the east end of the National Mall on Capitol Hill gives the U.S. Capitol away. The U.S. Capitol is also considered to be an museum. Inside, an eager visitor can find many examples of American art and history. The U.S. Capitol is an symbol of a American government.

Try It
Write a paragraph with five sentences about a local landmark. Once you have finished your paragraph, underline the articles.

Answers will vary.

43

Review: Common Nouns, Proper Nouns, Regular Plurals, Irregular Plurals, Subject Pronouns, Object Pronouns, Pronoun Agreement

Putting It Together
Answer the following questions by circling the letter of the best answer.

1. Which sentence contains a common noun?
   a. I visited Yellowstone National Park.
   b. I liked seeing the animals.
   c. I heard that you went to Everglades National Park.

2. Which sentence contains a proper noun?
   a. The U.S. Capitol is in Washington D.C.
   b. History is one of my favorite subjects.
   c. I like to study science.

3. Which sentence contains a regular plural noun?
   a. I liked seeing the moose at the park.
   b. The geese were in the pond and then they flew overhead.
   c. The cats liked playing together.

4. Which sentence contains an irregular plural noun?
   a. The dogs loved playing in the water.
   b. Rabbits make great pets.
   c. The mice scurried under the floorboards.

5. Which sentence contains a subject pronoun?
   a. Ava went on a science field trip.
   b. She went on a science field trip.
   c. Aaron went on a science field trip.

6. Which sentence contains an object pronoun?
   a. The team captain picked me.
   b. The team captain picked Sandy to play.
   c. He picked the best player to be on his side.

7. Which sentence has an incorrect use of pronoun agreement?
   a. The brothers left his jackets on the field.
   b. Diane picked up her books at the library.
   c. Jason forgot his books at the library.

44

Review: Regular Past Tense Verbs, Irregular Past Tense Verbs, Action Verbs, Helping Verbs, Linking Verbs, Verb Agreement

Draw a line from the word or phrase in Column A with the word or phrase that it describes in Column B.

Column A	Column B
1. sound	Past Tense Regular Verb
2. The books are heavy.	Past Tense Irregular Verb
3. should	Action Verb
4. taught	Helping Verb
5. whispered	Linking Verb
6. throw	Subject/Verb Agreement

Review: Adjectives, Adverbs, Conjunctions, Interjections, Prepositions, Articles

Write the part of speech above the words in bold. Write **ADJ** for adjectives, **ADV** for adverbs, **CONJ** for conjunctions, **INT** for interjections, **PREP** for prepositions, and **ART** for articles.

INT
Hurray! Happy Birthday!
ADV   PREP ADJ   ART   ART
Birthdays were **first** celebrated **in ancient** Rome. **The** Romans celebrated **the**
PREP   ADJ   CONJ ADJ   ART   PREP
birthdays **of** their **favorite** gods **and important** people, like **the** emperor. **In** Britain, they
ART ADJ   PREP ART   ART   PREP   CONJ
celebrate **the Queen's** birthday. **In the** United States, **the** birthdays **of** presidents **and**
ADJ   ADJ   ART   PREP ART ADJ   PREP PREP
important leaders, like Martin Luther King, are celebrated. **In** Japan, Korea, **and** China,
ADV   ADJ   ART   ART PREP   PREP
the **sixtieth** birthday marks **a** transition **from an active** life **to** one of contemplation.
PREP ART ADJ   ART PREP   PREP   ART ADJ
Many Eastern cultures don't even recognize **the actual** date **of** birth. When **the first**
PREP ART ADJ   ADV ADV
moon **of the new** year arrives, everyone is **one year** older.

45

Page 46

Declarative sentences are sentences that make statements. They say something about a place, person, thing, or idea. When punctuating a declarative sentence, use a period at the end of the sentence.

> Henry Bergh was the founder of the American Society for the Prevention of Cruelty to Animals.
> Pizza is my favorite food.
> Marathons are 26.2 miles long.

Identify It
Place a check mark in front of each declarative sentence. Leave the other sentences blank.

1. __✓__ Venice is a city in Italy.
2. __✓__ Venice has a network of canals used for transportation.
3. _____ Have you ever been to Venice?
4. __✓__ The Grand Canal is the main thoroughfare.
5. __✓__ Three bridges cross the Grand Canal.
6. _____ How many bridges cross the Grand Canal?
7. _____ Look at the beautiful bridge!
8. __✓__ Venice has a very temperate climate.
9. _____ How warm does it get in Venice in the summer?
10. __✓__ Venice is one of the most beautiful cities in Europe.

46

Page 47

Proof It
Make sure that each declarative sentence ends in a period. If the punctuation is correct, place a check mark before the sentence. If not, use the proofreading marks to make each declarative sentence end with a period.

> ⊙ – inserts periods
> ℓ – deletes punctuation

1. __✓__ I want to play baseball tomorrow.
2. _____ I can't wait to go to the gym with Greg and Sarah℣⊙
3. __✓__ If you order pizza, make sure to get onions.
4. __✓__ Do you see the rainbow?
5. _____ Jen said that it is time to eat℣⊙

Try It
Write a dialogue between two people. Write ten sentences about a place they are visiting. Be sure to use periods when you are making declarative sentences.

Answers will vary.

47

Page 48

Interrogative sentences are sentences that ask questions. When punctuating an interrogative sentence, use a question mark.

> Did I see lightning in the sky?
> Do you like fresh spinach in your salad?
> Do you run in the morning or in the evening?

Complete It
Complete the following sentences by circling the correct punctuation.

1. Alla walked briskly five times around the block (.)?
2. Did you see the famous statue on your vacation (. (?)
3. The spider spun a beautiful web (.)?
4. Did the poem inspire your artwork (. (?)
5. How quickly did you complete the obstacle course (. (?)
6. The designer showed great style (.)?
7. I like the rhythm of that song (.)?
8. Did your dad make spaghetti for dinner last night (. (?)
9. Are you going to try out for the wrestling team (. (?)
10. Do you lift weights to strengthen your muscles (. (?)
11. Are those chestnuts I smell roasting (. (?)
12. My friends are coming over after dinner (.)?
13. I think the batteries are dead in that radio (.)?
14. Aren't the pictures in the museum beautiful (. (?)
15. Where are you going after school (. (?)
16. Who is at the door (. (?)
17. Jon and I walked around the block (.)?
18. The baseball game starts at seven o'clock tonight (.)?
19. What time did you say (. (?)
20. Arlene and Beth joined a book club (.)?

48

Page 49

Solve It
A farmer is taking a student on a tour of his garden. The student has many questions about what kind of vegetables he grows. The farmer's answers are given, but the student's questions are missing. Write the question with the appropriate punctuation in the space provided. The first one has been done for you.

1. How many vegetables do you grow?   I grow many vegetables.
2. _What vegetable do you grow the most?_   I grow mostly soy beans.
3. _What is your favorite vegetable?_   My favorite vegetable is broccoli.
4. _What should I study if I want to be a farmer?_   If you want to be a farmer, you should study many subjects, but especially science, math, and social studies.

Try It
Write a list of questions you might ask a local business owner.

Answers will vary.

49

Answer Key

Exclamatory sentences are sentences that reveal urgency, strong surprise, or emotion. When punctuating an exclamatory sentence, use an exclamation mark.

    I can't believe you ate the whole pie!
    Look at how much weight he is lifting!
    I think I smell a skunk!

Only use exclamation points when expressing urgency and strong surprise or emotion. Exclamation marks can also be used in dialogue, when the character or speaker is making an urgent or emotional statement.

Identify It
Identify which sentences are exclamatory by putting an exclamation mark at the end of the sentences. If it's not exclamatory, leave it blank.

1. Watch out for the ice !
2. Ouch! I can't believe I stubbed my toe on the table again !
3. Where are you having dinner tonight
4. The storm is quickly coming our way !
5. I'm not sure if I want to go to the movies or not
6. It is so cold I think I have frostbite !
7. Don't you like the cold weather
8. Ah! The sunset is gorgeous !
9. You're it !
10. Oh no! The bridge is out !
11. What time is it
12. Oranges are my favorite fruit
13. Watch out! The oranges fell off the display !
14. The Lord of the Rings is my favorite series of books
15. That author really inspires me !

> Except for interrogative sentences, answers may be subjective. Accept all reasonable answers.

50

Rewrite It
Read the following postcard from one friend to another. The writer seems excited about her trip, but doesn't express it in her writing. Rewrite the postcard changing declarative sentences to exclamatory ones.

> Dear Linda,
>
> I'm having a wonderful time in Florida. The weather is fantastic. It's been sunny every day. We went swimming in the hotel's pool on Tuesday. Then, on Wednesday, we actually swam in the ocean. Tomorrow we are going to visit a marine animal sanctuary. Do you remember studying about the rescued marine animals in school? I can't wait to see the fish and animals. I wish you were here. See you soon.
>
> Drew

> Changes are subjective except for the interrogative sentence. Accept all reasonable changes.

Try It
Write a postcard to a friend or relative about a trip you have taken recently. Make it exciting by including exclamatory sentences. Make sentences exclamatory when you really want them to stand out.

> Answers will vary.

51

Imperative sentences demand that an action be performed. The subjects of imperative sentences are usually not expressed. They usually contain the understood subject *you*. Imperative sentences can be punctuated with a period or an exclamation mark. Use an exclamation mark in the same instances as you would for an exclamatory sentence, such as expressing urgency, surprise, or strong emotion.

    Look at the rabbit behind the trees.
    (*You* look at the rabbit behind the trees.)

    Write the note here.
    (*You* write the note here.)

    Throw me the ball!
    (*You* throw me the ball!)

Complete It
Choose a verb from the box that will complete each imperative sentence and write it on the line provided. Remember, the subject *you* is implied in the sentences.

carry	drive	pick	swing	vote
drink	pass	shoot	throw	yell

1. _Vote_ for Simon for president!
2. _Pass_ the potatoes, please.
3. _Pick_ up the paper from the floor.
4. _Carry_ that bag for your aunt.
5. _Throw_ the ball to second base!
6. _Drive_ slowly when on ice.
7. _Swing_ the racket higher.
8. _Yell_ the cheers louder!
9. _Drink_ all of your tomato juice.
10. _Shoot_ the basketball through the hoop!

52

Find It
Use a thesaurus to find other imperative words that are synonyms of the imperative words below.

1. call - _____
2. carry - _____
3. drink - _____
4. drive - _____
5. look - _____
6. pass - _____
7. pick - _____
8. run - _____
9. shoot - _____
10. stop - _____

> Answers will vary. Accept all reasonable responses.

Try It
Write ten imperative sentences using the synonyms from the activity above. Remember to use correct punctuation.

1. _____
2. _____
3. _____
4. _____
5. _____
6. _____
7. _____
8. _____
9. _____
10. _____

> Answers will vary.

53

Answer Key

Simple sentences are sentences with one independent clause. Independent clauses present a complete thought and can stand alone as a sentence. Simple sentences do not have any dependent clauses. Dependent clauses do not present a complete thought and cannot stand alone as sentences.

Simple sentences can have one or more subjects.
> The *costumes* glittered.
> The *costumes* and the *jewelry* glittered.

Simple sentences can have one or more **predicates**, or verbs.
> The costumes *glittered*.
> The costumes *glittered* and *sparkled*.

Simple sentences can have more than one subject and more than one predicate.
> The *costumes* and the *jewelry glittered* and *sparkled*.

Identify It
Underline the subject or subjects in the following simple sentences.

1. Elsa, Tanya's mom, liked baking cookies.
2. Elsa liked baking cookies and cooking spaghetti.
3. Elsa and Tanya liked baking and cooking together.
4. Elsa liked baking and cooking.
5. Elsa liked baking better.
6. Tanya liked baking and cooking.
7. Tanya liked cooking better.
8. Tanya liked eating her mom's cookies.
9. Elsa liked eating her daughter's spaghetti.
10. Tanya's friends liked coming to dinner.

54

Identify It
Underline the predicate or predicates in the following simple sentences.

1. Elsa, Tanya's mom, liked baking cookies.
2. Elsa liked baking cookies and cooking spaghetti.
3. Elsa and Tanya liked baking and cooking together.
4. Elsa liked baking and cooking.
5. Elsa liked baking better.
6. Tanya liked baking and cooking.
7. Tanya liked cooking better.
8. Tanya liked eating her mom's cookies.
9. Elsa liked eating her daughter's spaghetti.
10. Tanya's friends liked eating cookies and spaghetti.

Try It
Write ten simple sentences of your own. Remember, simple sentences may have more than one subject and more than one predicate.

Answers will vary.

55

Compound sentences are sentences with two or more simple sentences (independent clauses) joined by a coordinate conjunction, punctuation, or both. As in simple sentences, there are no dependent clauses in compound sentences.

A compound sentence can be joined by a comma and a coordinate conjunction.
> The costumes glittered, *but* the jewelry was dull.

A compound sentence can also be two simple sentences joined by a semicolon.
> The costumes glittered; the jewelry was dull.

Match It
Match simple sentences in Column A with simple sentences in Column B to create compound sentences. Add either a comma with a coordinate conjunction or a semicolon.

Column A	Column B
1. The seats were bad.	The snack bar line was long.
2. The actors were funny.	We can stay late.
3. The intermission was short.	The show was good.
4. The ushers were nice.	...cket takers were rude.
5. We can leave	...rchestra played well.
6. The theater lights were low.	The actors were serious.
7. The audience laughed.	The audience applauded.
8. The actors' voices were loud.	The seats were sold out.
9. The play had good reviews.	The music was soft.
10. The actors bowed.	The stage lights were bright.

Answers will vary.

56

Solve It
Combine each pair of simple sentences into a compound sentence.

Simple Sentences

1. Richard likes apples. Jackie likes pears.
2. Jackie likes skating. Richard likes running.
3. Richard likes dancing. Jackie likes singing.
4. Jackie likes summer. Richard likes winter.
5. Richard likes math. Jackie likes science.

Compound Sentences

1. _____
2. _____
3. _____ Answers will vary.
4. _____
5. _____

Try It
Continue to write about what Richard and Jackie each like and don't like. Write three more sentences for each character. Then, combine the sentences to form compound sentences.

Richard

_____ Answers will vary.

Jackie

_____ Answers will vary.

Compound Sentences

_____ Answers will vary.

57

Complex sentences have one independent clause and two or more dependent clauses. The independent and dependent clauses are connected with a subordinate conjunction or a relative pronoun. Remember, dependent clauses do not present a complete thought and cannot stand alone as sentences. The dependent clause can be anywhere in the sentence.

Common subordinate conjunctions include *after, although, as, because, before, if, since, when, where, while, until,* and *unless.*

One complex sentence (connected with subordinate conjunction):
    Since he got a math tutor, his math grades have improved.

The independent and dependent clauses can also be connected with relative pronouns like *who, whose, which,* and *that.*

One complex sentence (connected with relative pronoun):
    Mr. Addy, *who* is a math teacher, tutors Ashton.

Combining simple sentences into complex sentences adds variety and clarity to writing.

Identify It
Circle the letter that best answers each question.

1. Which of the following sentences contains two simple, individual sentences?
   a. He is wearing his baseball uniform. He is holding his baseball bat.
   b. He is wearing his baseball uniform and holding his baseball bat.
   c. He is wearing his baseball uniform, although the game was cancelled.

2. Which of the following sentences contains a compound sentence?
   a. She is eating a salad. She is drinking lemonade.
   b. She is eating a salad, and she is drinking lemonade.
   c. She is drinking lemonade, since she is thirsty.

3. Which of the following sentences contains a complex sentence?
   a. Mary went jogging. Rose went jogging.
   b. Mary and Rose went jogging.
   c. Before breakfast, Mary and Rose went jogging.

4. Which of the following sentences contains a complex sentence?
   a. Mike was learning about moose at school. Mike was learning about caribou at school.
   b. Mike and Gil were learning about arctic animals at school.
   c. Mike, who loved animals, was learning about moose and caribou at school.

58

Rewrite It
Rewrite the following article combining simple sentences to make compound and complex sentences.

    Why would a ten-week old piglet wander the streets of New York City? New York City animal control officers asked the same question. One Friday afternoon they found a tiny piglet. They thought she had escaped from a market. They took her to a shelter. She was treated for wounds on her legs. She was treated for a respiratory infection. The shelter staff named her Priscilla. A local sanctuary took her in. They treated her. She was quite sick. Now she is healthy. Priscilla was adopted by a family in Michigan. She loves her new home.

Answers will vary.

Try It
Write an article about an event in your school using compound and complex sentences. Include at least three complex and two compound sentences in your article.

Answers will vary.

59

A **sentence fragment** is a group of words that is missing either a subject or a verb. A sentence fragment is also a group of words that doesn't express a complete thought, as in a dependent clause.

    Takes a walk every day at lunch. *(no subject)*
    Complete Sentence: *Sandy* takes a walk every day at lunch.

    A walk every day at lunch. *(no subject and no verb)*
    Complete Sentence: *Sandy takes* a walk every day at lunch.

    Since the line was so long. *(not a complete thought)*
    Complete Sentence: *We went to a different restaurant,* since the line was so long.

Match It
The sentences in Column A are sentence fragments. Choose a group of words from Column B that will complete the sentence and make it whole. Write the new sentences on the line.

Column A	Column B
1. is the twelfth month of the year.	December has two birthstones,
2. Until 46 B.C.,	December
3. Several European countries	Orville Wright made the first heavier-than-air flight at Kitty Hawk, North Carolina
4. turquoise and zircon.	celebrate December 6th as the Feast of Saint Nicholas.
5. on December 17, 1903.	December had only 29 days.

1. December is the twelfth month of the year.
2. Until 46 B.C., December only had 29 days.
3. Several European countries celebrate December 6th as the Feast of Saint Nicholas.
4. December has two birthstones, turquoise and zircon.
5. Orville Wright made the first heavier-than-air flight at Kitty Hawk, North Carolina on December 17, 1903.

60

Identify It
Now that you have completed the 5 sentences, identify why the sentences in Column A are fragments. Write *missing a subject, missing a verb,* or *missing a subject and a verb.*

1. missing a subject
2. missing a subject and a verb
3. missing a verb
4. missing a subject and a verb
5. missing a s subject and a verb

Try It
When is your birthday? Write ten complete sentences about the month of your birth. Make sure all of your sentences are complete, with a subject, a verb, and express complete thoughts. Once you have completed your sentences, circle the subjects and underline the verbs.

1.
2.
3.
4.
5.
6.   *Answers will vary.*
7.
8.
9.
10.

61

Combining short, choppy sentences into longer more detailed sentences makes writing much more interesting and much easier to read. Sentences can be combined in a variety of ways.

Compound subjects and compound verbs:

Brad went on a hiking trip. C.J. went on a hiking trip.
Brad and C.J. went on a hiking trip.

We hiked on our long weekend away. We biked on our long weekend away.
We *hiked and biked* on our long weekend away.

Adjectives and adverbs:

I ate an orange for breakfast. The orange was sweet.
I ate a *sweet orange* for breakfast.

Abby walked through the foggy forest. Abby walked slowly.
Abby *walked slowly* through the foggy forest.

Making complex sentences (using subordinate conjunctions):

The class was going on a camping trip. They were going on the trip providing it didn't rain.
The class was going on a camping trip *providing it didn't rain.*

Rewrite It
Rewrite these simple sentences into compound or complex sentences.

1. Rachel went to the carnival on Saturday. Dan went to the carnival on Saturday.
   Rachel and Dan went to the carnival on Saturday.
2. The popcorn crackled as it popped. The popcorn snapped as it popped.
   The popcorn cracked and snapped as it popped.
3. Nancy investigated the old trunk. Nancy investigated the brown trunk.
   Nancy investigated the old, brown trunk.
4. Carson excitedly spoke about his journey. Carson loudly spoke about his journey.
   Carson excitedly and loudly spoke about his journey.
5. We can stop for breakfast. We can stop for breakfast if it is quick.
   We can stop for breakfast, as long as it is quick.

62

Identify It
Draw a line to match the sentences on the left with the type of combined sentences they are on the right.

1. So that the birthday party remains a surprise, we must get there on time. — compound subjects
2. Helen and Tammy brought sweaters as presents. — combining adjectives
3. Helen brought a purple, knit sweater. — complex sentence

4. Ginger liked raspberry, lemon cake. — compound verbs
5. Because it was her birthday, Ginger's mom baked her favorite cake. — combining adjectives
6. Ginger's mother cooked and baked for hours. — complex sentence

7. Ginger and her friends had a great time at the party. — compound subjects
8. Ginger greatly appreciated the presents. — combining adverbs
9. Although it was late, the friends stayed for more cake. — complex sentence

Try It
Pretend that you are a reporter covering a birthday party. Write an account of the party. Use adjective and adverbs and both compound and complex sentences.

Answers will vary.

63

Match It
Circle the letter of the best answer in each of the following questions.

1. Which of the following sentences makes the best topic sentence?
   a. Pat was on a journey.
   b. Pat started on his journey with only his pack on his back.
   c. Pat had a backpack.
2. Which of the following topic sentences is the beginning of a descriptive paragraph?
   a. The day started out bright and sunny.
   b. School cafeterias should be open before and after school hours.
   c. Building a bookcase can be fast and easy.
3. Which of the following sentences is a sentence from the middle of a paragraph?
   a. A recycling program should be started in our school for three reasons.
   b. Recycling helps the environment.
   c. Recycling will benefit us all.
4. Which of the following sentences is from a narrative paragraph?
   a. The bears can weigh up to 800 pounds.
   b. Littering is unsanitary and inconsiderate.
   c. Pat journeyed many days and many nights.

Try It
Write a short descriptive, narrative, expository, or persuasive paragraph. After you have chosen your topic, use the first section to write a rough draft of your paragraph. Use the second section to rewrite your paragraph with all corrections and revisions made.

Answers will vary.

65

Review: Declarative Sentences, Interrogative Sentences, Exclamatory Sentences, Imperative Sentences

Putting It Together
Identify the following sentences. After each sentence, write if the sentence is *declarative, interrogative, exclamatory,* or *imperative.*

1. Walk up the steps and then turn left. __imperative__
2. Anne took a risk and accepted the new job. __declarative__
3. Was that statue priceless? __interrogative__
4. Our team won the game in the final two seconds! __exclamatory__

Review: Simple Sentences, Compound Sentences, Complex Sentences, Sentence Fragments, Combining Sentences

After each sentence, write whether it is a *simple sentence,* a *compound sentence,* a *complex sentence,* or a *sentence fragment.* If the sentences are simple sentences or sentence fragments, rewrite them as compound or complex.

1. Edward and Cynthia wrapped and delivered the presents. compound sentence
2. Although it was a sunny day, sentence fragment
   Although it was a sunny day, it was cold outside.
3. The coach challenged her team. The coach inspired her team. simple sentences
   The coach challenged and inspired her team.
4. Grill the peaches until they are slightly brown. complex sentence
5. The ocean was blue. The ocean was warm. simple sentences
   The ocean was blue and warm.
6. After the hike, sentence fragment
   After the hike, we sat down to rest.

Accept any reasonable answer for number 2 and 6.

66

Answer Key

The following paragraph is out of order. Reorder the sentences so they make sense. Rewrite the paragraph and then write what kind of paragraph it is.

It also protects our natural habitats. We should all be committed to a recycling program. The same is true with curbside pollution; less trash means less trash and pollution on our streets. Recycling greatly reduces our need for landfills. It also reduces curbside pollution. When we cut down trees, birds, squirrels, rabbits, and many other forest animals lose their homes. Recycling is important to our environment for many reasons. These are excellent reasons why we should encourage our friends and family to recycle. If we recycle the paper products we use, fewer trees will have to be cut down. Recycling saves trees. If we recycle what would be trash, there will be less garbage to put into the landfills.

Recycling is important to our environment for many reasons. Recycling saves trees. If we recycle the paper products we use, fewer trees will have to be cut down. It also protects our natural habitats. When we cut down trees; birds, squirrels, rabbits, and many other forest animals lose their homes. Recycling greatly reduces our need for landfills. If we recycle what would be trash, there will be less garbage to put into the landfills. It also reduces curbside pollution. The same is true with curbside pollution; less trash means less trash and pollution on our streets. These are excellent reasons why we should encourage our friends and family to recycle. We should all be committed to a recycling program.

Persuasive

67

The names of cities, states, and countries are considered **proper nouns** and are always capitalized.

Capitalize the names of cities:
Anchorage   Columbus   Kona   Detroit   Los Angeles   New York

Capitalize the names of states:
Alaska   Ohio   Hawaii   Michigan   California   New York

Capitalize the names of countries:
United States   Mexico   Japan   Denmark   Israel

Do not capitalize the words *city*, *state*, or *country* in a sentence. These words are common nouns.

Complete It
Circle the correct answer in each of the following sentences.

1. The capital of California is (Sacramento) sacramento).
2. This (City, (city) has a population of approximately 407,000.
3. (Los Angeles, los angeles), has the largest population in California.
4. The city in the United States with the largest population is (New York) new york).
5. The (City, (city) of New York has a population of approximately 22 million.
6. The capital city of the state of (New York) new york) is Albany.
7. Albany, (New York) new york) has a population of approximately 40,800.
8. The largest city in (California) california) is Los Angeles.
9. California is the most populated (State, (state) in the United States.
10. The least populated state in the United States is (Wyoming) wyoming).
11. China is the most populated (Country, (country).
12. The population of (China) china) is over 1.2 billion.
13. The population of the (United States) united States) is over 293 million.
14. The largest continent, Asia, is made up of 48 (Countries, (countries).
15. Australia is the only continent that is its own (Country, (country).

68

Proof It
Proofread the following journal entry. Use the proofreading marks to correct capitalization errors.

≡ – capitalizes a letter
/ – lowercases a letter

Today was my fourth day in Europe. We have been traveling quickly. I feel like I'm a long way from my home in athens, Ohio. We started our trip in London, england. We saw Big Ben and the Tower of London. Then we took the tube to paris, france. We climbed the Eiffel Tower – what an awesome view! We also saw the Mona Lisa at The Louvre Museum. France is a beautiful Country. Then it was off to belgium. We started our tour in the City of Brugges. I have eaten many waffles in ohio, but I've never seen as many as in this Country. Tomorrow we leave belgium for munich, germany. I'm hoping to eat one of those big pretzels while I'm there. I know next year I'm taking an eating tour of Europe.

Try It
Write a journal entry about a city you have visited. Be sure to name the state, if it applies, and the country.

Answers will vary.

69

Days of the week and months of the year are considered **proper nouns** and are always capitalized.

Capitalize days of the week:
Sunday   Monday   Tuesday   Wednesday   Thursday   Friday   Saturday

Capitalize months of the year:
January   February   March   April   May   June
July   August   September   October   November   December

Solve It
The following sentences each contain the name of a day of the week. However, the sentences don't make sense. Unscramble the names of the days of the week so the sentences make sense. Write the day on the line after each sentence. Remember to capitalize the day of the week.

1. dswdeayen falls in the middle of the week. ___Wednesday___
2. The day ryifda got its name from the German word *frigga*. ___Friday___
3. The sun gave its name to nysuda. ___Sunday___
4. hsruydta was named for Thor, a god in northern mythology. ___Thursday___
5. On onmayd, the day of the moon, I go to school. ___Monday___
6. I play baseball on suartyad, the first day of the weekend. ___Saturday___
7. Tiw's day gives its name to usedtay, honoring the northern mythological wrestler Tir. ___Tuesday___

70

(calendar image with January through December)

Answer Key

Complete It
Complete the following sentences by writing the correct month of the year on the line. Remember to capitalize the month when you write it in. Use an encyclopedia or the Internet if you need help.

1. The chrysanthemum is the flower for **November**, the eleventh month of the year.
2. The United States celebrates Independence Day on **July** 4th.
3. **February** is the shortest month of the year.
4. In the Northern Hemisphere, summer begins in the month of **June**.
5. **August** was named for the Roman emperor, Augustus.
6. Fools come out to play on this **April** day.
7. The month of **January** was named for the Roman god, Janus.
8. *Cinco de Mayo* is a holiday celebrated in Mexico on the fifth day of **May**.
9. The sapphire is the birthstone for **September**, the ninth month of the year.
10. Farmers start to bring in their crops, including pumpkins, in the month of **October**.
11. In the Northern Hemisphere, winter begins in the month of **December**.
12. It is often said that the month of **March** "Comes in like a lion and goes out like a lamb."

Try It
Write an advertisement announcing a garage sale you are going to have. Include the days of the week, dates, place, and time in your ad. Be sure to correctly capitalize all of the proper nouns.

Answers will vary. Check that all proper nouns are correctly capitalized.

71

The names of specific streets, places, and people are proper nouns and are capitalized.
Capitalize the names of specific streets.
Stanley Street   Ohio Avenue   Crosswinds Boulevard

When using the nonspecific words like *street* and *road* in a sentence, they are not capitalized.
I live one *street* over from you.
Capitalize the names of specific places.
Rocky Mountain National Park

Capitalize the first and last names of people, including special titles, initials, and abbreviations that go with the names.
President Jimmy Carter

Do not capitalize nonspecific street names, places, or titles when used without a name in a sentence.
My best friend is going to run for class president.

Identify It
Write **PN** if the sentence has a proper noun. If not, leave it blank.

1. **PN** Felicia and Bryan stayed at the Lake Hotel on their vacation.
2. _____ Drive slowly on this street, many children play here.
3. **PN** Dr. Edwards gave my kitty a pill that will make her feel better.
4. _____ The hotel where we stayed was beautiful.
5. **PN** Cross over Breeze Loop and then turn right on Riverbend Drive.
6. _____ The president of our class will speak at the rally.
7. **PN** Hawaii Volcanoes National Park is located on the island Hawaii.
8. _____ The park has many attractions.
9. _____ The doctor was kind to her patients.
10. **PN** Karl lives on Lane Road.
11. **PN** The bridge connected Mill Drive to Shamrock Road.
12. **PN** Dr. Green is a wonderful veterinarian.

72

Proofread the following paragraph using proofreading marks. Look for errors in the use of capitalization with proper nouns.

= – capitalizes a letter
/ – lowercases a letter

Do you believe in haunted houses? How about haunted hotels? Granville, Ohio is home to the buxton inn. The buxton inn, located on broadway street, has a haunting reputation. The hotel was built in 1812 by orrin granger, founder of the city of Granville. The hotel was named after major buxton, who ran the inn from 1865–1905. So who's ghost has appeared in this inn? orrin granger was first seen in the 1920s eating a piece of pie in the kitchen. major buxton has been seen by guests, mostly in the dining room. The ghosts of other owner's have also been spotted. Even a kitty of days gone by has been seen roaming throughout the buxton inn. Of course the ghost cat now has a name – Major Buxton.

Try It
Write a short autobiography. Write about the city where you were born, the name of the first street where you lived, your parents' and siblings' names, and the name of your first school and first teacher. Write about a few of your favorite memories growing up. Make sure all of the proper nouns in your autobiography are capitalized.

Answers will vary.

73

Words like *mother, father, aunt*, and *uncle* can be used as **proper nouns** or **common nouns**. When they are used as proper nouns, they should be capitalized.

The words *mother* and *father* can be used in place of name. If they are, they are capitalized.
Mother, where did I leave my jacket?

In the following instance, *father* is not used as a replacement of a name.
My *father* took me to the hockey game.

The same is true for the words *aunt, uncle, grandmother*, and *grandfather*.
Aunt Clara has a wonderful cat.
My *aunt* likes to travel in the mountains.
I like to play catch with *Uncle Richard*.
My *uncle* was great in sports when he was in school.

Official names, such as those of businesses and their products, are capitalized. Nonspecific names of products are not capitalized, even if they follow the business or product name.
Papa's Pizza (name of business)
I like *Papa's Pizza's* pizza. (business name followed by product name)

Match It
Circle the letter that matches the description.

1. the word *mother* not used to replace a name
   a. Mother, please pass the beans.
   b. My mother was the pitcher on her softball team.
2. the word *grandfather* used as a name
   a. Grandfather Clarence was a veterinarian.
   b. My grandfather is a good cook.
3. the word *aunt* not used to replace a name
   a. My aunt has the cutest puppy.
   b. Aunt Marilyn is a teacher.
4. official business name followed by product name
   a. Oat Crisps cereal
   b. Oat Crisps
5. official business name without product name
   a. Tender Pet pet food
   b. Tender Pet

74

Answer Key

Solve It
Fill in the missing information on this family tree. Be sure to capitalize proper names. Write three different sentences about the people on this tree.

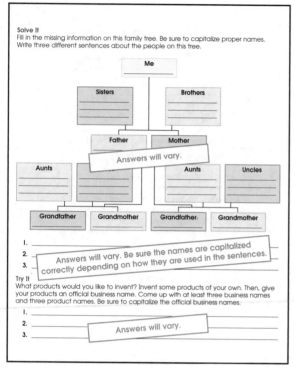

Me

Sisters

Brothers

Father   Mother

Answers will vary.

Aunts   Aunts   Uncles

Grandfather   Grandmother   Grandfather   Grandmother

1. _____
2. _____   *Answers will vary. Be sure the names are capitalized*
3. _____   *correctly depending on how they are used in the sentences.*

Try It
What products would you like to invent? Invent some products of your own. Then, give your products an official business name. Come up with at least three business names and three product names. Be sure to capitalize the official business names.

1. _____
2. _____
3. _____   *Answers will vary.*

75

Titles are **proper nouns** and are capitalized. The first and last words of titles are always capitalized, as well as every word in between except for articles (*a, an, the*), short prepositions (*in, of, at*), and short conjunctions (*and, but*). These words, however, should be capitalized if they are the first word in the title. Most titles are also underlined in text. Song titles and essays, however, are in quotes.

This rule applies to titles of the following: books, newspapers, magazines, articles, poems, songs, plays, movies, works of art, pictures, stories, and essays.

book: *Catcher in the Rye*	play: *The Music Man*
movie: *Master and Commander*	work of art: *Mona Lisa*

School subjects are capitalized if they name a specific course.
My favorite course is *Literature and Poetry*.

Do not capitalize the names of general subjects.
My *math* teacher is also the baseball coach.

Exception: Language subjects are all proper nouns, so they should all be capitalized. I am studying my *French* homework.

Complete It
Circle the correct answer that completes each of the following sentences.

1. I read (The Lord of the Rings) the Lord Of The Rings) series during summer vacation.
2. I like doing the crossword puzzle in the (Chicago tribune, Chicago Tribune).
3. My favorite song is ("Drops of Jupiter") "drops of jupiter").
4. Have you ever seen (Raiders of The lost Ark, Raiders of the lost Ark)?
5. I have gym class after (spanish, Spanish).
6. Mr. Howard is the best (history, History) teacher.
7. Mr. Hayes teaches a course called (Geometry, geometry).
8. Can I walk with you to (Math, math) class?
9. My sister is studying (American poetry, american poetry) in college.
10. The poem ("Dawn", "dawn") by Paul Lawrence Dunbar is one of Dylan's favorites.

76

Rewrite It
These reviews have errors in capitalization. Make the corrections as you rewrite them.

* Sleeper of the Year! The movie Happy Times In Snoozeville is for you if you need a nap. The dialogue is boring, the action is slow, and the actors can't act. Don't waste your money on this dud.

* Great Read! The perfect Peach is just what it says—a peach. Take this book to the beach or read it in your favorite armchair. The perfect Peach has rich characters and a comforting mood. Don't miss this great read.

* Ouch! My Ears! What was Kay Joe thinking when she recorded "Dancing in the desert"? She can't hit the high notes and the lyrics make no sense. The track "Singing On The Seas" is worth the money—but buy the single.

Sleeper of the Year! The movie Happy Times in Snoozeville is for you if you need a nap. The dialogue is boring, the action is slow, and the actors can't act. Don't waste your money on this dud.

Great Read! The Perfect Peach is just what it says – a peach. Take this book to the beach or read it in your favorite armchair. The Perfect Peach has rich characters and a comforting mood. Don't miss this great read.

Ouch! My Ears! What was Kay Joe thinking when she recorded "Dancing in the Desert"? She can't hit the high notes and the lyrics make no sense. The track, "Singing on the Seas," is worth the money – but buy the single.

Try It
Write the title of your favorites below. Don't forget to capitalize when necessary and underline or use quotes correctly.

book _____   magazine _____
movie _____   *Answers will vary.*
song _____   play _____

77

The first word of every **sentence** is capitalized.
Build the parfait by sprinkling the berries on the yogurt.

The first word in **direct quotations** is capitalized. Quotation marks are used to show the exact words of a speaker, a direct quotation. The quotation marks are placed before and after the exact words.

Our teacher said, "*Please* go to the board and write your answer."
"*I* hope I know the answer," I whispered as I walked to the board.

Indirect quotations are not capitalized. An indirect quotation does not use the exact words of a speaker and does not use quotation marks.
The coach said he wanted to have practice three nights a week.

If a quotation is split and the second half continues, do not capitalize the second half. If a new sentence begins after the split, then capitalize it as you would with any sentence.
"I think my puppy is the cutest in the class," said the boy, "*and* the best trained."
"My aunt took me to the shelter to get a kitty," said Candy. "*We* found the perfect calico!"

Identify It
One of the sentences in each of the following pairs is not capitalized correctly. Write an X on the line before the sentence that is capitalized correctly.

1. __X__ The apartment was perfect for Phyllis and Marc.
   _____ the apartment was perfect for Phyllis and Marc.
2. __X__ "Check out the exercise room," said Maria. "It has everything we use."
   _____ "Check out the exercise room," said Maria. "it has everything we use."
3. _____ The agent John said The pool will open in the spring.
   __X__ The agent John said the pool will open in the spring.
4. __X__ "Rob," said Regina, "the view is fantastic!"
   _____ "Rob," said Regina, "The view is fantastic!"
5. _____ Eddy and Jackie decided They would move next month.
   __X__ Eddy and Jackie decided they would move next month.

78

Page 79

Use the proofreading marks to correct the errors in capitalization.

| ≡ - capitalizes a letter |
| / - lowercases a letter |

"Hey, Mom," hollered Matt on his way in the house, "G̲uess what I learned about in school today?"

Matt knew his mother wouldn't guess. He said H̲e would show her. h̲e pulled a picture out of his backpack.

"Here it is, Mom," said Matt. "I̲t's a snot otter!"

"Oh my," exclaimed his mom, "W̲hat exactly is a snot otter?"

"I knew you would ask," Matt gleefully replied. "S̲not otters are a type of salamander. T̲hey live in cool, fast moving streams with big rocks. They live up to 29 years. But their habitats are declining."

"That is sad," replied Matt's mother. "W̲hy are they in danger?"

"Water pollution and sediment build-up in streams are a couple of reasons they are in danger," answered Matt. "I̲f someone finds a snot otter, it should be put back in the stream. They are not pets."

"Well, I'm glad to hear that," Matt's mom said smiling.

Try It
Write a dialogue about a student telling a teacher about an animal. Pay attention to the capitalization of sentences in and outside of dialogue.

Answers will vary.

79

Page 80

A **personal letter** has five parts: heading, salutation, body, closing, and signature. Personal letters have special punctuation.

The **heading** of a personal letter is the address of the person writing the letter and the date it is written. The name of the street, city, state, and month are all capitalized.
    3126 Milly Dr.
    Marblehead, MI 20000
    October 5, 2006

The **salutation** is the greeting and begins with *dear*. Both *dear* and the name of the person who is receiving the letter are capitalized. Place a comma after the name.
    Dear Stanley,

The **body** is the main part of the letter and is capitalized just like all sentences and paragraphs.

The **closing** can be written many ways. Only the first word is capitalized. Place a comma after the closing.
    Your friend,   Sincerely,   All the best,

The **signature** is usually only your first name. It is always capitalized.
    Milton

Proof It
Proofread the personal letter. Use the proofreading marks to make corrections in capitalization.

| ≡ - capitalizes a letter |
| / - lowercases a letter |

                    5711 E̲astwind L̲oop
                    A̲nchorage, AK 20000
                    F̲ebruary 26, 2008

D̲ear A̲unt Linda,

How have you been? I've been great. S̲chool is going very well this year. I really like social studies and E̲nglish. However I've had a little trouble with math. M̲y best friend is helping me with that.

I'm playing on the junior varsity basketball team. I love it. I think I will try out for the track team this spring.

I can't wait to see you on your next visit. Please tell U̲ncle Ray I said hello.

                    With L̲ove,
                    Kay

80

Page 81

Try It
Write a personal letter. Be sure to capitalize the letter correctly. Use the information provided on page 80 if you need help setting your personal letter up correctly.

Answers will vary.

81

Page 82

Review: Proper Nouns: Cities, States, Countries, Days of the Week, Months of the Year, Names of Streets, Places, People, Words Used as Names, Official Names, Titles, Names of Subjects, Sentences, Direct Quotations, Personal Letters

Putting It Together
Proofread the following personal letter. Make all of the necessary capitalization corrections. Then, use the following page to rewrite the letter.

| ≡ - capitalizes a letter |
| / - lowercases a letter |

                    4064 P̲alm T̲ree L̲ane
                    O̲akdale, FL 20000
                    March 19, 2008

D̲ear Perry,

How do you like A̲naheim, C̲alifornia? Do you like your new school? T̲hings are about the same here. I'm getting ready for the baseball season. Our first game is next T̲hursday. C̲oach Baum says T̲hat I can start as pitcher.

The basketball team won the division, but we didn't get very far in state. I think the baseball team will do well. W̲e already have a sponsor for the team. Fast Feet Sporting Goods has already signed on. I like Fast Feet Shoes, but I'm still going to buy my gloves from your U̲ncle's store.

My family is going on vacation this summer. We're going to C̲hicago, I̲llinois. My G̲randpa and Grandma are going, too. We are going to visit A̲unt Christina. We're also going to the N̲avy P̲ier and the S̲ears T̲ower. Did you know that the Sears Tower used to be the tallest B̲uilding in the world?

Are you trying out for the track team this year? Aren't try-outs in M̲arch? I hope you get to come back to visit soon. M̲aybe we can meet somewhere in the middle next winter break? Write when you can.

                    Y̲our Friend,
                    Denny

82

Answer Key

83

Answers will vary.

84

Declarative and imperative sentences both use **periods**. A declarative sentence makes a statement. An imperative sentence demands an action be performed, and the subject is usually not expressed. Sometimes, an imperative sentence can end with an exclamation point.

> They left for their trip on Friday.
> Look at the icicle formations on the roof!

Quotation marks are used to set off direct quotations in dialogue. Quotation marks are placed before and after the direct quotation. A period is placed at the end of a direct quotation sentence when it is declarative or imperative. The period goes inside the quotation mark.

> Lori said, "I'll give the ticket to the agent."

In direct quotation sentences when the quote comes at the beginning of the sentence, use a comma at the end of the direct quotation instead of a period.

> "I'll give the ticket to the agent," said Lori.

Complete It
Add the correct punctuation mark in each sentence.

1. "My house is on the right," said Martha.
2. Martha said, "My house is on the right."
3. "Look at the bright plants my mom planted."
4. "My house has plants like that!" Deidre replied.
5. Deidre continued, "We also have some bushes mixed in, too."

85

Proof It
Proofread the following paragraphs. Use proofreading marks to make punctuation corrections.

> ℓ - deletes letters, words, punctuation
> ∧ - inserts letters, words, punctuation

"Cities, like cats, reveal themselves at night," said the British poet Rupert Brooke. Perhaps he didn't realize how true his statement is. Some cats save their owners' lives when they reveal themselves at night.

Take, for example, Aggie. Aggie was a cat rescued from a shelter when she was five weeks old. Aggie was curious and playful, but not aggressive. That is until one evening when she heard an intruder trying to climb through the front window. Before her owners even made it downstairs, she pounced, attacked, and scared away the intruder.

Cats also rescue and save their own. One particular cat lived in an abandoned building with her five recently born kittens. When the building caught on fire what was she to do? Of course she had to save her family. One by one she carried her kittens out of the burning building to safety. She was burned and blistered but she got every one of her kittens out. The firefighter who made sure the cat and kittens were safe and cared for is now known as "The Animal Guy."

Try It
Interview a friend about his or her pet. Then, write a newspaper article about it. Be sure to include direct quotations.

Answers will vary.

86

The **period** is used in more than just sentences. Periods are used in abbreviations, initials, and titles before names.

Use a period after each part of an abbreviation. Do not leave a space between the period and the following letter.
> B.C.   A.D.   B.A.

Use a period after each letter of an initial.
> Michael J. Fox   J. K. Rowling   J. R. R. Tolkien

Use a period with abbreviated titles before names.
> Dr.   Mr.   Mrs.

Do not use periods if the abbreviation is an acronym. **Acronyms** are words formed from the first letters of words in a phrase.
> NATO (North Atlantic Treaty Organization)

Match It
Draw a line to match the following abbreviations, titles, and acronyms in Column A with their meanings in Column B.

Column A	Column B
B.S.	Public Broadcasting System
DJ	United Nations International Children's Education Fund
PBS	District Attorney
D.A.	Disc Jockey
SCUBA	Mister
D.V.M.	Doctor of Veterinary Medicine
UNICEF	Bachelor of Science
Mr.	Self-contained underwater breathing apparatus
M.D.	Bachelor of Arts
B.A.	Medical Doctor

Answer Key

Rewrite It
The following people were either misidentified or are not pleased with how their names appeared in a recent magazine article. Rewrite them as they request.

1. Donna Kay Dell — "I prefer my middle name to be an initial."
   Donna K. Dell
2. Melissa Sarah Oliver — "I prefer first and middle initials."
   M. S. Oliver
3. Dr. E. Bates, Ph.D. — "I am a medical doctor."
   Dr. E. Bates, M.D.
4. M. L. Roberts — "I am a doctor."
   Dr. M. L. Roberts, M.D.
5. Steven Paul Starks — "I would like my first name as an initial."
   S. Paul Starks

Try It
You are having a formal party. Make a formal list of ten people you would like to invite. Include their titles and abbreviations, like Mr., Dr., Mrs., and M.D.

Answers will vary.

87

Interrogative sentences ask questions and they are followed by **question marks**.
How many students are in the class?

When used in quotations, questions marks can be placed either inside or outside of the end quotation mark depending on the meaning of the sentence.

When the question mark is punctuating the quotation itself, it is placed inside the quote.
The customer asked, "How much does the car cost**?**"

When the question mark is punctuating the entire sentence, it is placed outside the quote.
Did the sales person say, "It's the most expensive car on the lot"**?**

A question mark is unnecessary in sentences with indirect quotations.
I asked my sister if she would help us with our math homework.

Complete It
Place a question mark in the appropriate place in the sentences that need one. In the sentences that do not use a question mark, place a period at the end of the sentence.

1. Did you hear back from the admission's office?
2. Jason said he saw the movie 12 times.
3. My mom asked, "How much homework do you have tonight?"
4. Did your teacher say, "Finish the entire chapter tonight"?
5. I asked Jill if she had a good day.
6. There must have been 200 people in the theatre.
7. The hiker asked, "Is this as far as this trail goes?"
8. The server asked if we wanted dessert.
9. Are you going to play tennis with your sister this evening?
10. Dr. Eric said to take the medicine once a day.
11. My brother asked, "Is Judy studying with you after school?"
12. Did the coach say, "Run three more laps"?

88

Proof It
Proofread the following dialogue. Make corrections using proofreading marks. Look for errors with question mark use.

- deletes letters, words, punctuation
- inserts letters, words, punctuation
- moves punctuation from one place to another

Patrick was doing a report on the Milky Way Galaxy. He asked the director of the local observatory if he could ask him some questions.

Patrick asked, "How many planets orbit the sun in our solar system?"

The director answered, "We have nine planets that orbit the sun."

Patrick asked, "Was my teacher right when she said planets are divided into two categories?"

"Yes, Patrick, Mrs. Sanchez was right," said the director. "Mercury, Venus, Earth, Mars, and Pluto belong to the terrestrial planets." The director asked, "Do you know the name of the other category?"

"The other category is the Jovian planets?" answered Patrick.

The director said, "You are correct!"

Patrick had a good time and learned a lot about the Milky Way Galaxy. He asked the director if he could come back again.

Try It
Choose a subject you would like to know more about. Write a dialogue between you and your teacher. Ask your teacher questions about the subject you chose. Have your teacher ask you questions in the dialogue, too.

Answers will vary.

89

Exclamatory sentences are sentences that express surprise and strong emotion and are punctuated with **exclamation points**.
I'm so excited you made it into the first college on your list!

Interjections sometimes require exclamation points.
Oh, no! I left my homework at home!

Identify It
Identify which sentences should have exclamation points. Place an **X** at the end of each sentence that needs an exclamation point.

1. Watch out The stove is hot __X__
2. The soup should be on medium high _____
3. Thank you for my beautiful flowers __X__
4. Tulips are my favorite flower _____
5. Ouch My fingers were still in the door __X__
6. After all my hard work, I finally got an A on the test __X__
7. I have a lot of homework to do tonight _____
8. I won the race __X__
9. Oh, no The rain is coming down really hard now __X__
10. I like the sound of rain on the rooftop _____
11. The cars are coming fast __X__
12. My favorite color is green _____
13. The ice is slippery __X__
14. Don't shut the door before getting your keys _____
15. Wait I forgot the keys __X__

Answers may vary.

90

Answer Key

Page 91

Solve It

Which of the following situations would require an exclamation point? Write a short sentence for each illustration you see. Include interjections and exclamation points when you think they are necessary.

Answers will vary.

Try It

Write six more sentences that should be written using exclamation points.

1. _____
2. _____
3. _____
4. _____   *Answers will vary.*
5. _____
6. _____

91

Page 92

Commas have a variety of uses. Three uses for commas are commas in a series, commas in direct address, and commas used with multiple adjectives.

A **series** is at least three items listed in a sentence in a row. The items can be words, phrases, or clauses. Commas are used to separate them.
I must clean the kitchen, the bathroom, and the family room this weekend.

When the name of a person spoken to is used in a sentence, it is called **direct address**. A comma is used to separate the name of the person from the rest of the sentence.
Sarah, after our chores are done, we can go to the park.

When more than one adjective is used to describe a noun, they are separated by commas.
The sweet, cool apple tasted good on the hot day.

Make sure each adjective describes the noun. There is no comma in the following sentence because the pizza is not piping. The adverb *piping* describes the adjective *hot*.
The piping hot pizza was ready to come out of the oven

Match It

Match the following sentences in Column A to the type of commas they require in Column B. Draw a line from Column A to Column B to make the match.

Column A	Column B
1. The soft, sweet, loving kitten purred.	commas in a series
2. They stayed out of the biting cold water.	commas in direct address
3. Daphne, please answer the door.	commas separating adjectives
4. I worked out on the treadmill, bike, and elliptical cycle.	no comma necessary

Column A	Column B
5. The sizzling hot sauce was too hot to eat.	commas in a series
6. Stephanie, please pass the strawberries.	commas in direct address
7. The sweet, juicy, ripe peaches were perfect.	commas separating adjectives
8. The tennis players grabbed their towels, bags, and balls on their way off the court.	no comma necessary

92

Page 93

Rewrite It

Rewrite the sentences, adding commas where necessary.

1. John wanted pasta vegetables and rolls for dinner.
   John wanted pasta, vegetables, and rolls for dinner.
2. Tiffany make the reservation for 7:30.
   Tiffany, make the reservation for 7:30.
3. The new black car was just what he wanted.
   The new, black car was just what he wanted.
4. I checked in on the slowly boiling water.
   I checked in on the slowly boiling water.
5. Keith had to do his homework eat dinner and take out the trash.
   Keith had to do his homework, eat dinner, and take out the trash.

Try It

Make a list of five of your favorite things. Then, make a list of words that describe these things. Write five sentences about your favorite things using the words that describe them. Be sure to include commas in the appropriate places.

1. _____   _____
2. _____   _____
3. _____   *Answers will vary.*
4. _____
5. _____   _____

93

Page 94

Use a **comma** to combine two independent clauses with a coordinate conjunction.
The players must be well trained, and they must train for at least six months.

If a sentence begins with a prepositional phrase, set it off with a comma.
After he finishes his homework, he can talk with his friends.

Commas are also used when setting off dialogue from the rest of the sentence.
The tour guide said, "Today's walking tour will take us past several museums."
"Then, we will eat in a cafe," promised the tour guide.

Complete It

Complete the following sentences by adding commas where necessary. Not all of the sentences need commas.

1. The Teton Mountain Range is a beautiful sight, and it is a challenge for rock climbers.
2. The Teton Mountain Range is located in Wyoming, and the range is in part of the Grand Teton National Park.
3. Because of its beauty, more than 3 million people visit each year.
4. Visitors have been known to say, "This is one of the most inspiring places I've seen."
5. Millions of people gaze at the peaks, yet it remains peaceful.
6. The range not only has more than 100 lakes, but also 200 miles of trails.
7. Rock climbers come from all over the world to climb Grand Teton.
8. "The view from the mountain is breathtaking," said one climber.
9. While Grand Teton's highest peek is 13,700 feet, other peaks attract climbers.
10. "Wildlife viewing is amazing here," said another tourist.

94

Answer Key

Proof It
Proofread the following paragraph. Add commas where necessary.

| ℓ – deletes letters, words, punctuation |
| ∧ – inserts letters, words, punctuation |

What is a marathon? Most runners know that a marathon is a foot race of 26.2 miles‸but not everyone knows how the marathon began. Now popular worldwide‸the marathon has its roots in Greece. We are familiar with bicycle couriers‸but ancient Greeks used foot couriers. Many of them had to run city to city to make deliveries. In 490 B.C.‸Persia was at war with Greece. A Persian army landed 25 miles from Athens at the city of Marathon. After a mighty battle‸the Greeks were victorious. A runner was sent from Marathon to Athens to spread the news of the victory. Pheidippides ran the 25 miles from Marathon to Athens. When he reached the city‸ legend says he said‸ "Rejoice, we conquer." Then, Pheidippides fell dead. Although the facts are not known for sure‸the legend prevails. The modern race got a name‸and the marathon was born.

Try It
Write a paragraph explaining your favorite sport, how it got its beginning, and why you like it. Use a variety of sentences. Add a quotation of your own.

Answers will vary.

95

The five parts of the personal letter are: **heading**, **salutation (greeting)**, **body**, **closing**, and **signature**. **Commas** appear in four of the five parts of the personal letter.

A **comma** follows the city and the date in the heading.
> 3151 Stuckey Lane
> Chicago, IL 30000
> March 7, 2008

A **comma** follows the name in the salutation.
> Dear Mary,

Follow the normal rules for using comma in sentences.

A **comma** follows the last word in the closing.
> Your friend,

Proof It
Proof the following friendly letter. Add commas where necessary.

| ◊ – inserts commas |

5512 Alpine Lane
Ridgeview‸CO 55214
April 26‸2008

Dear Marina‸

How are you? Are you getting excited for summer? I am going to volunteer at the local animal shelter‸and I am going to learn all about the different kinds of animals there. I am sure that it will be a hard job‸but it will be rewarding, too.

What are your plans for summer? Will you be going camping with your parents like you did last year? That sounds like so much fun! After you get back‸I want to know all about it.

I need to get back to reading about animal care‸and I hope to hear from you soon!

Your friend‸

Sharon

96

Try It
Write a friendly letter of your own. Pay attention to your use of commas.

Answers will vary.

97

Quotation marks are used to show the exact words of a speaker, called a **direct quotation**. The quotation marks are placed before and after the exact words.
> "I must make it to the post office before 5:00," said Sharon. "I want to get my invitations in the mail today."

Quotation marks are also used when a direct quotation is made within a direct quotation. In this case, single quotation marks are used to set off the inside quotation.
> Dylan said, "Michael, the coach said, 'Practice will be at 4:00 instead of 3:00.'"

The single quotation marks express what the coach said. The double quotation marks express what Dylan is saying as a direct quote.

Quotation marks are used with some titles. Quotation marks are used with the titles of short stories, poems, songs, and articles in magazines and newspapers.
> short story: "A White Heron"

If a title is quoted within a direct quotation, then single quotation marks are used.
> Hannah said, "I hope the DJ plays my favorite song, 'Purple People Eater.'"

Match It
Match the following sentences or titles from Column A to the type of quotation in Column B. Draw a line to make the match.

Column A	Column B
1. Susan said, "Let's go to lunch at 12:30."	direct quotation
2. "Prairie Island," Connie answered. "My boss said, 'Our lunch meeting is scheduled for 12:00 sharp.'"	quote within a quote
3. "Prairie Island"	title

Column A	Column B
4. "Soak Up the Sun"	direct quotation
5. My sister said, "The coach said 'Eat a good dinner the night before the game.'"	quote within a quote
6. "I'm heading for the beach," Sheryl said.	title

98

Page 99

Proof It
Proofread the following dialogue using proofreading marks. Make corrections on the use of quotation marks.

� – inserts quotations

"Claude Monet lived from 1840 to 1926. He was the founder of impressionism," said Mrs. Konikow.

"What is impressionism?" asked Doug.

"Impressionism is an art form that captures a visual image and uses colors to give the effect of reflected light. Many of Monet's paintings were landscapes," answered Mrs. Konikow.

"Did Mrs. Konikow say, 'Many of Monet's paintings were landscapes?'" asked Patricia.

"Yes," answered Doug, "landscapes are stretches of scenery that can be scene in one view."

"Like flower gardens?" asked Patricia.

"Yes, Patricia," said Mrs. Konikow, "like flower gardens. Later in his life, Monet retired from Paris and moved to his home in Giverny, France, where he continued to paint. He had beautiful gardens. You can see them in books and at his house in France."

"Someday, I would like to go to France," said Patricia, "but for now I think I'll just take a trip to the library."

Try It
Practice writing sentences with quotation marks. Write one sentence that is a direct quotation, one that is a quote within quotes, and one that includes a title.

1. _____
2. _____ Answers will vary.
3. _____

Page 100

Apostrophes are used to form contractions, possessives, and plurals.

Contractions are shortened forms of words. The words are shorted by leaving out letters. An apostrophe takes the place of the omitted letters.
   I am = I'm   let us = let's

Possessives show possession, or ownership. To form the possessive of a singular noun, add an apostrophe and an **s**.
   I have *Walt's* books.

To form the possessive of plural nouns ending in **s**, simply add the apostrophe. If the plural noun does not end in an **s**, add both the apostrophe and an **s**.
   The *boys'* uniforms will be ready on Friday.
   The *children's* puppet show will be performed on Wednesday.

If you are writing about more than one letter of the alphabet or number, only add **s** to form the plural.
   My name has two B**s** in it.
   I have two page 4**s** in my book.

Complete It
Complete the following sentences by changing words to contractions. Write the contraction on the line that follows the words.

We're	It's	He'd
I'm	We've	let's

1. (I am) _____I'm_____ hungry and thirsty.
2. (We are) _____We're_____ on our way to the café.
3. (It is) _____It's_____ not too far away, and it has the best muffins.
4. Do you think we should take something back for Pablo? (He would) _____He'd_____ appreciate it.
5. (We have) _____We've_____ a lot of homework to do at lunch.
6. Come on, (let us) _____let's_____ hurry.

Page 101

Solve It
Look at the pictures below and write a sentence for each that identifies the object and who the object belongs to. The first one has been done for you.

1. Answers will vary.
2. The kitty's treats are in a foil bag.
3. The runners' shoes are muddy.
4. The chef's vegetables are fresh.
5. The tourists' map is big.

Try It
Write how many letters are duplicated in the following names. Then, on the last line, write your name. Write how many letters are duplicated in your name. The first one has been done for you.

1. Nathan 2 Ns and 2 As
2. Lee 2 Es
3. Greg 2 Gs
5. David 2 Ds
4. Marjorie 2 Rs
6. Answers will vary.

Page 102

Colons are used to introduce a series, to set off a clause, for emphasis, and in time.

Colons are used to introduce a series in a sentence. Usually, but not always, the list is proceeded by the words *following, these, things*.
   The chef does the *following*: washes the vegetables, chops the vegetables, and steams the vegetables.

Colons are sometimes used instead of a comma, in more formal cases, to set off a clause.
   The weather reporter said: "We can expect six more inches of snow overnight."

Colons are used to set off a word or phrase for emphasis.
   We hoped to see some activity in the night sky. And then we saw it: *a shooting star*.

Colons are used when writing the time.
   Are we meeting at 9:00 or 10:00?

Identify It
Identify why the colon is used in each sentence. Write a **S** for series, **C** for clause, **E** for emphasis, or **T** for time.

1. __E__ One of the most violent storms occurs primarily in the United States: tornados.
2. __C__ A tornado is defined as the following: "a violent rotating column of air extending from a thunderstorm to the ground."
3. __S__ Thunderstorms that develop in warm, moist air in advance of a cold front can produce these things: hail, strong wind, and tornados.
4. __T__ Tornados are most likely to occur in the spring and summer months between 3:00pm and 9:00pm, but can occur anytime.
5. __S__ Staying aware is most important for safety. During storms, look for the following: dark, greenish skies, large hail, loud roars, and flash floods.
6. __C__ You can be prepared by doing the following: developing a safety plan, practicing house drills, and listening to weather reports.

Page 103

Rewrite It
Rewrite the following passage, adding colons where needed.

> I would like to apply for the following position Latin Cultural Food Writer. I graduated from the Culinary Art Institute in New York. I have cooked dishes from many cultures Latin, French, and Middle Eastern.
>
> I have expertise in Mexican food history, culture, and cooking. When the Spanish explorer Cortez first came to America he found many culinary surprises chocolate, peanuts, vanilla, beans, squash, avocadoes, coconuts, corn, and tomatoes. I have created many dishes which incorporate many of these foods and flavors.
>
> Included with this letter are the following my resume, school transcripts, and references.
>
> You can reach me weekdays between 7 00am and 3 00pm.

I would like to apply for the following position: Latin Cultural Food Writer. I graduated from the Culinary Art Institute in New York. I have cooked dishes from many cultures: Latin, French, and Middle Eastern.
I have expertise in Mexican food history, culture, and cooking. When the Spanish explorer Cortez first came to America he found many culinary surprises: chocolate, peanuts, vanilla, beans, squash, avocadoes, coconuts, corn, and tomatoes. I have created many dishes which incorporate many of these foods and flavors.
Included with this letter are the following: my resume, school transcripts, and references.

Try It
Write four sentences, one for each type of colon use: series, clause, emphasis, and time.

1. _____
2. _____
3. _____ Answers will vary.
4. _____

Page 104

A **semicolon** is a cross between a period and a comma. Semicolons can be used to join two independent clauses, to separate clauses containing commas, and to separate groups which contain commas.

Semicolons join two independent clauses when a coordinate conjunction is not used.
The loud thunder scared me; I hid under my covers.

Semicolons are used to separate clauses when they already contain commas.
Although the thunder was loud, it did no harm; I emerged from my bed safe and sound.

Semicolons are also used to separate words or phrases that already contain commas.
We are looking for the following features in our new house: *a garage with space for two cars, storage, and tools; a kitchen with a refrigerator, dishwasher, stove, and microwave; and bedrooms with closets and a bathroom.*

Match It
Match the first half of the sentences in Column A with the second half in Column B. Then, circle all of the semicolons in the sentences.

Column A
1. Donna was close to home;
2. After the game was over, my team went for pizza;
3. The long shopping list included the following:
4. I didn't go to school;
5. Because we were on vacation, we weren't home to get the call;
6. Before sending the resume do the following:

Column B
- I went to the doctor instead.
- it wasn't important anyway.
- she had traveled a long way.
- check the spelling, facts, and names; call your references; and verify the address.
- we were all starving.
- rye, pumpernickel, and wheat bread; lettuce, carrots, and onions for salad; and cranberry, grapefruit, and tomato juice.

Page 105

Proof It
Proofread the following magazine article using proofreading marks. Look for missing and out of place semicolons, and commas used instead of semicolons.

- ℯ – deletes letters, words, punctuation
- ⌃ – inserts semicolon

Who is Sue? Sue is a Tyrannosaurus rex; she is the largest and best preserved T-rex ever discovered. Although she was discovered in South Dakota, Sue now resides in Chicago, Illinois, at The Field Museum; she is on display for the public to see. Visitors can see up close Sue's features: ribs, forelimbs, and mouth bones; CT scan of her skull; the braincase; as well as many other parts. Sue is quite special; she is the most complete T-rex fossil ever discovered. While we have a lot to learn about our past from Sue, we may also learn about our present and future; Sue has given us much to explore.

Try It
Write four complete sentences each with two independent clauses joined by a semicolon.

Answers will vary.

Page 106

Hyphens are used to divide and to create new words.

Use a hyphen to divide the word between lines. Divide words between syllables.
sanctu-ary   de-posit

Do not divide a one syllable word or words with fewer than six letters.
ball, toy, cedar, book

Divide syllables after vowels if a vowel is a syllable by itself.
cele-brate   not: cel-ebrate

Do not divide one letter from the rest of the word.
ele-phant   not: e-lephant

Hyphens can be used to create new words when combined with *self, ex,* or *great.*
My *great-grandfather* worked on the railroad.

Solve It
Solve the following puzzle. Place the words from the box in the appropriate spaces. The words must be divided correctly in order to fit into the boxes.

| basket | compose | dinosaur | graduate | puppy |
| bicycle | crocodile | embankment | personal | television |

1. tele - vision
2. bas - ket
3. per - sonal
4. croco - dile
5. gradu - ate
6. com - pose
7. embank - ment
8. bicy - cle
9. puppy
10. dino - saur

Answer Key

Proof It
The words in this advertisement are broken in the wrong places. Use the proofreading marks to correct the placement of the hyphens.

- deletes letters, words, punctuation
∧ - inserts letters, words, punctuation
↩ - moves punctuation from one place to another

Come and see what's wild in Alaska. Anchorage, A-
laska, in South central Alaska, is home to a wide variety of wildlife.
Anchorage is one of the best cities in the world to view nat-
ure and wildlife at its best. All year long, you are able to see wildlife
such as: moose, caribou, bears, dall sheep, wolves, whales, ly-
nx, and otters. At the Alaska Wildlife Conservation Center, you can see
wildlife in a special environment. The Alaska Wildlife Conservation Center is a non-profit organization that serves as a refuge for
orphaned, injured, and ill animals. The center also educates visitors about Alaskan wildlife. The Tony Knowles Trail; a biking, hiking,
and ski trail that runs through Anchorage, is also an excellent viewing spot
for wildlife. Just be careful, we are invading their homes. Treat all animals you see with respect, and with distance. Come and take a walk
on our wild side. Visit Anchorage, Alaska!

Try It
How many *self*'s, *ex*'s, and *great*'s can you think of? Write at least two of each that start with these prefixes and a hyphen. Use a dictionary if you need help.

1. _____   7. _____
2. _____   8. _____
3. _____
4. _____   Answers will vary.
5. _____   11. _____
6. _____   12. _____

107

Parentheses are used to show extra material, to set off phrases in a stronger way than commas, and to enclose numbers.

Supplementary, or extra, **material** is a word or phrase that gives additional information.
Those apples *(the ones in the basket)* are good for baking in cobblers.

Sometimes, words or phrases that might be set off with commas are set off with parentheses, instead. It gives the information more emphasis for a stronger phrase.
The television program, *the one that was canceled*, was my favorite.
The television program *(the one that was canceled)* was my favorite.

Parentheses are also used to enclose numbers in a series.
I do not want to go to the movie because *(1)* it is too late, *(2)* it is all the way across town, and *(3)* it is too scary.

Complete It
Complete the following sentences by adding parenthetical phrases from the box to the sentences. Add the parentheses where they belong. The first one is done for you.

(1) (2) (3) with four doors	(1) (2) (3) my best friend	my great-great-grandmother see key

1. The road on this map looks like a two-lane road.
   The road on this map (see key) looks like a two-lane road.
2. The recipe is the best!
   The recipe (my great-great-grandmother's) is the best!
3. Andy is moving to another state.
   Andy (my best friend) is moving to another state.
4. I love to exercise because it is good for my heart, it gives me energy, and I feel good afterward.
   I love to exercise because (1) it is good for my heart, (2) it gives me energy, and (3) I feel good afterward.
5. The new, blue car is the one I want.
   The new, blue car (with four doors) is the one I want.
6. Pigs are my favorite animal because they are intelligent, cute, and make "oinking" sounds.
   Pigs are my favorite animal because they are (1) intelligent, (2) cute, (3) make "oinking" sounds.

108

Rewrite It
Rewrite the following paragraph. Add parentheses as needed.

The Japanese Tea Ceremony is an ancient and beautiful ritual. The ceremony is 1 a way of preparing tea, 2 a way of serving tea, and 3 a way of drinking tea. The room where the tea ceremony is held is the teahouse called *chashitsu*. One particular tea ceremony *Chaji* is held to honor guests into a home. The guests 1 enter the tea house from the garden called *roji*, 2 are served a light meal, 3 take a short break in the garden, 4 return to the tea house. At this time, the host 1 prepares a thick tea called koicha, and 2 prepares a thin tea. Lafcadio Hearn an author of books about Japan and Japanese fairy tales said, "The tea ceremony requires years of training and practice... yet the whole of this art, as to its detail, signifies no more than the making and serving of a cup of tea."

The Japanese Tea Ceremony is an ancient and beautiful ritual. The
ceremony is (1) a way of preparing tea (2) a way of serving tea and
(3) a way of drinking tea. The room where the tea ceremony is held is
the teahouse (called chashitsu). One particular tea ceremony is held
to honor guests into a home. It is very structured and ritualistic. The
guests (1) enter the tea house from the garden (called roji), (2) are
served a light meal, (3) take a short break in the garden, (4) return to
the tea house. At this time the host (1) prepares a thick tea (called
koicha), and (2) prepares a thin tea. When the host and guests are
finished, they respectfully acknowledge each other. Lafcadio Hearn
(an author of books about Japan and Japanese fairy tales) said, "The
tea ceremony requires years of training and practice... yet the whole
of this art, as to its detail, signifies no more than the making and
serving of a cup of tea."

Try It
Write one sentence that has supplemental material in parentheses, one sentence that sets off information with emphasis, and one sentence that has numbers and parentheses.

1. _____
2. _____   Answers will vary.
3. _____

109

Review: Periods: After Declarative and Imperative Sentences, In Dialogue, In Abbreviations, In Initials, Titles Before Names, Question Marks, Exclamation Points

Putting It Together
The following sentences are missing punctuation. Add periods, question marks, and exclamation points where needed.

1. Don't forget to stop by the store and pick up bread on your way home from school.
2. What time is Gillian stopping over?
3. Helen said, "The flowers in my garden are beautiful."
4. Look out!
5. J.R.R. Tolkien is my favorite author.
6. My dentist is Dr. Guten.
7. Do I have an appointment with Dr. Guten on Tuesday?
8. Ellen Hobbs, M.A. is speaking at our school on Friday.

Review: Commas: Series, Direct Address, Multiple Adjectives, Combining Sentences, Set-Off Dialogue, Personal Letters

Proofread the following letter. Add commas where necessary using proofreading mark.

∧ - inserts commas

6919 Muirfield Rd.
Bloomfield MI, 30000
September 23, 2008

Dear Carl,

I wanted to write you and tell you about my weekend. I went to the Ryder Cup, and I saw my favorite players! The Ryder Cup is a golf match between the United States and Europe. It is the only team golf match with a real history. I got to see Tiger Woods, Sergio Garcia, and Jay Haas. Although you can't say anything during the course of play, I yelled out, "Tiger you're the best!" between holes. It was great. I bought you a hat at the gift shop and I'll give it to you when I see you winter break. I hope you are well.

Your friend,
Mindy

110

Spectrum Language Arts
Grade 5

Answer Key

Page 111

Review: Quotation Marks, Apostrophes, Colons, Semicolons, Hyphens, Parentheses

Rewrite each sentence. Add punctuation where necessary.

1. My great grandmother played softball in college, said Aidan.

   "My great-grandmother played softball in college," said Aidan.

2. The doctor said "You'll be fine!"

   The doctor said, "You'll be fine!"

3. I want to take Ms. Roses class because 1 she teaches a lot of geography, 2 she takes her classes on field trips, and 3 she is nice.

   I want to take Ms. Rose's class because (1) she teaches a lot of geography, (2) she takes her classes on field trips, and (3) she is nice.

4. "Charlotte, did our teacher say, the bus for the museum leaves at 9 00?"

   "Charlotte, did our teacher say, 'The bus for the museum leaves at 9:00'?"

5. I am excited about going to the museum of art I want to be an artist someday.

   I am excited about going to the museum (of art); I want to be an artist someday.

6. Susan got what she had been hoping for a new job.

   Susan got what she had been hoping for: a new job.

7. I didnt read the series, The Lord of the Rings, but I loved the movies.

   I didn't read the series, The Lord of the Rings, but I loved the movies.

111

Page 112

The **present tense** of a verb tells that the action is taking place now or continuously.
    Ted and Parker *come* over every day after school.
    I *do* the crossword puzzles on Sunday.
    Can I *go* with you to the library now?

The **past tense** of a verb tells that the action took place in the past.
    Cassie *came* with us to the movies last weekend.
    I not only *did* the crossword puzzle last Sunday, I *did* the word search, too.
    Renee and Kristen *went* on an archeological dig last semester.

The **past participle** of a verb tells that the action began in the past and was completed in the past. In order to form the past participle, the verb must be preceded by one of the following verbs: *was, were, has, had,* or *have.*
    Karen, Lori, and Blair *had come* with us on our vacation three years in a row.
    The chef checked to see if the cake *was done.*
    Adam *had gone* to see that same movie many times.

Solve It
Find all of the forms of *come, do,* and *go* in the puzzle. The verbs that go with the past participles are also included. The words can be horizontal, vertical, diagonal, backward, and forward.

come	did	went	has
came	done	gone	is
do	go	had	was

112

Page 113

Complete It
Complete the following sentences by circling the correct verb in parentheses.

1. Timmy (come, **has come**) over for dinner every night this week.
2. I can (did, **do**) my homework now.
3. The class (go, **had gone**) to the same exhibit last year.
4. Please (came, **come**) and pick up your order.
5. Andrea (do, **has done**) that assignment many times before.
6. The butterflies (**had come**, has come) back to this same location for many years.
7. Lynne and Nicole (gone, **went**) to see the butterflies at the butterfly house.
8. Meg (did, **was done**) with her chores before the programs started.
9. Ollie (came, **come**) home from his vacation with many pictures.
10. Beth and Eddie (**go**, gone) to the same vet as Eric and Shane.

Try It
Practice writing the present, past, and past participle forms of the verbs *come, do,* and *go.* Write one sentence of each type for each verb.

Answers will vary.

113

Page 114

The **present tense** of a verb tells that the action is taking place now or continuously.
    Bob and Nelly *run* every day at lunch.
    I *see* the stars and even some planets with this telescope.
    Come and *sit* beside me for dinner.

The **past tense** of a verb tells that the action took place in the past.
    Mike and Jim *ran* together on the high school track team.
    Erica and Karen *saw* the play from first row seats.
    The kitten *sat* on the chair closest to the window.

The **past participle** of a verb tells that the action began in the past and was completed in the past. In order to form the past participle, the verb must be preceded by one of the following verbs: *was, were, has, had,* or *have.*
    The coach *has run* the track many times himself.
    John realized after he sat down that he already *had seen* the film.
    Mr. Chat couldn't believe he *had sat* on his hat.

Match It
Draw a line to match the verbs in Column A with its part of speech in Column B.

<u>Column A</u>   <u>Column B</u>

1. has run ——— present
2. saw ——— past
3. sit ——— past participle

4. sat ——— present
5. was seen ——— past
6. run ——— past participle

114

Answer Key

Proof It
Proofread the following paragraph. Use the proofreading marks to correct errors with the use of the verbs *run*, *see*, and *sit*. Use clues from the rest of the sentence as to what the tense of the sentence should be.

Answers will vary. Some answers are subjective.

~ deletes letters, words, punctuation

run
They have ran, follow, sniff, have seen, and sometimes they sit. They are an
                    see
important member of many teams. Who are they? They are rescue dogs. Rescue dogs
are important to police departments, fire departments, and many rescue organizations.
                            saw   have seen
Rescue dogs can see and smell things human beings can't. Human rescuers see these
         have run
dogs had run through wilderness looking for missing persons, sniffing for clues along
           sit
the way. Some dogs ran up snowy mountains to find fallen hikers and skiers. Sometimes
        have sat
they have sat for hours waiting for their turn to seek and rescue. And when they are
called, they are ready to go.
                                                                          run
    Rescue dogs and their guardians are well trained teams. They work together, ran
          have
together, play together, and rescue together. These teams go through many hours of
intensive training and see and experienced many types of challenging situations. We
owe a lot to these hard-working dogs and those who train and love them.
    Many believe that rescue dogs run with their noses to the ground in order to pick
                                                                          run
up scents. It's not necessarily true; rescue dogs can be trained to receive scents from
                      run
the air and can ran with noses up!

Try It
Practice writing the present, past, and past participle forms of the verbs *run*, *see*, and *sit*. Write one sentence of each type for each verb.

Answers will vary.

115

Adjectives modify, or describe, nouns. **Comparative adjectives** compare two nouns, and **superlative adjectives** compare three or more nouns.

cute/cuter/cutest   big/bigger/biggest   light/lighter/lightest

Describing one noun:
   Phoebe has a *cute* puppy.
   Melissa has a *big* dog.
   That truck carries *light* cargo.

Comparing two nouns:
   My pink sweater is *cuter* than my yellow one.
   Joe's sandwich is *bigger* than Barney's.
   Lance's bicycle is *lighter* than Greg's.

Comparing three or more nouns:
   Those are the *cutest* puppets I've ever seen.
   The house on the corner has the *biggest* snowman.
   My windbreaker is the *lightest* jacket in my closet.

Complete It
Complete the following sentences by circling the correct word or words in parentheses.

1. Of the three bats, Henry's is the (light, (lightest)).
2. Christina has a very ((cute), cuter) kitten.
3. My notebook is ((bigger), biggest) than yours.
4. ((Light), Lightest) rain fell on the roof.
5. Every mother thinks her child is the (cute, (cutest)) in the class.
6. After playing soccer, Aaron has a ((big), bigger) appetite.
7. I think the cartoon at 8:30 is ((cuter), cutest) than the cartoon at 8:00.
8. Jordan's bookbag is ((lighter), lightest) than Riley's.
9. Gillian wants to ride on the ((big), bigger) roller coaster in the park.
10. Aubrey drew her parents a ((cute), cuter) picture.
11. Adam has a ((bigger), biggest) lead in the race than Lewis.
12. Of all the boxes, Joe picked the (lighter, (lightest)) to carry.

116

Proof It
Proof the body of the following letter, replacing the incorrect form of the adjectives.

~ – deletes letters, words, punctuation
^ – inserts letters, words, punctuation

Dear Margie,
                                                                st
    Today was the best day of my trip to England. I saw the cute show of all. It was a
                                        st
marionette show. Marionettes are cute, puppet-like figures. They are lightest and small
                                                                            st
and operated by strings. Stages for performances by people are biggest than for
marionette shows, so I sat up close. I learned that puppet theatres have been popular
                                                            gest
for centuries in Europe, Asia, and America. It was the big form of entertainment for
                                                                      st
Europeans in the Middle Ages. I think the little children marionettes are cute, but the
                                  st
animal marionettes are the cute of all. Let's see a show together when I get home!

        Your friend,
        Barbie

Try It
Write a paragraph describing a performance you have seen. Use at least six adjectives from this lesson.

Answers will vary.

117

The word *more* before an adjective means it is **comparative**, comparing two nouns. The word *most* before an adjective means it is **superlative**, comparing three or more nouns. The words *more* and *most* are usually used instead of *er* and *est* with adjectives that have more than two syllables.
   Students in the morning class are *more energetic* than students in the afternoon class.
   Please sign the three forms in yellow first; they are *most important*.

If you don't know whether to use **er/est** or *more/most*, then say the words out loud. Use the form that sounds best.

Two adjectives do not follow either pattern for making comparative and superlative adjectives. The adjectives *good* and *bad* have their own rules.
   This is *good* strawberry ice cream.
   The strawberry ice cream is *better* than the chocolate ice cream.
   The strawberry ice cream is the *best* ice cream of all.

   That was a *bad* movie.
   The movie was *worse* than the one we saw last week.
   The movie we saw two weeks ago was the *worst* movie of all.

Identify It
Identify each of the following sentences as either a comparative sentence or a superlative sentence. Write **C** for comparative and **S** for superlative. Then, underline the adjectives (including the words *more* or *most*) in the sentences.

1. __S__ The most challenging sports competition in the world is the Tour de France.
2. __S__ The Tour de France can be ridden in some of the worst weather conditions.
3. __S__ One of the best shirts to earn in the Tour de France is the polka-dot jersey.
4. __S__ Lance Armstrong is one of the world's most famous bicyclers.
5. __C__ Lance Armstrong now has had more specialized training than he did years ago.
6. __C__ He is now a better rider than he was years ago.

118

Answer Key

Solve It
The following sentences are not finished. Use the pictures to help you solve the sentences. Write *more, most, good, better, best, bad, worse,* or *worst* in the blanks to solve each sentence. Each word will be used once.

1. I like my ice cream cone ____better____ than your ice cream cone.

2. This is the ____worst____ banana in the bunch.

3. That was a ____good____ book.

4. Paula has ____more____ pencils than Paul.

5. Alice has a ____bad____ cold.

Try It
Write your own sentence for each of the following adjectives: *good, better, best, bad, worse,* and *worst.*

Answers will vary.

119

Adverbs modify verbs, adjectives, and other adverbs. Some adverbs are easily confused with adjectives.

Bad is an adjective and *badly* is an adverb. Determine what you are modifying before using *bad* and *badly.*

A *bad* storm is heading our way.
Bad is used as an adjective modifying the noun *storm.* No **ly** is added.

Cami sings *badly.*
Badly is used as an adverb modifying the verb *sings.* Use the **ly** form of bad.

Good is an adjective and *well* is an adverb. Determine what you are modifying before using *good* and *well.*

Claudia is a *good* cook and bakes *well,* too.
In this sentence, the adverb *well* modifies the verb *bakes.* The adjective *good* modifies the noun *cook.*

The words *very* and *really* are both adverbs.

Please talk *very* softly in the library.
The adverb *very* modifies the adverb *softly* that modifies the verb *talk.*

Complete It
Complete the following sentences by circling the correct adverb in parentheses. Underline the verb, adjective, or adverb that it modifies. Then, write what type of word it modifies: **V** for verb, **ADJ** for adjective, **ADV** for adverb, and **N** for noun.

1. __V__ Jim was sick and so <u>ran</u> (bad, (badly)) during the race.
2. __V__ Amy had a great day and <u>ran</u> (good, (well)) in her race.
3. __N__ The <u>day</u> I lost the race was a ((bad,) badly) day for me.
4. __ADJ__ I was a (bad, (badly)) <u>beaten</u> runner.
5. __N__ But it was a ((good,) well) <u>day</u> for my friend.
6. __V__ She <u>accepted</u> her praises (good, (well)).
7. __V__ I will train harder so I do (good, (well)) in my next race.
8. __N__ That will be a ((good,) well) day for the whole team.

120

Proof It
Proofread the following article using proofreading marks. Look for errors with adjectives and adverbs. When you come to the adverbs *really* or *very,* underline the words they modify.

> ◦‿ - deletes letters, words, punctuation
> ∧ - inserts letters, words, punctuation

Where do you go to find the very best in wildlife viewing? The answer varies greatly. Well viewing can be found all over the United States. One particular wildlife refuge is good hidden. The Arctic National Wildlife Refuge is located in northern Alaska on the Bering Strait. You can only reach it by bush plane. But the travel is worth it with well sightings of caribou, wolves, grizzly and black bears, musk oxen, polar bears, and wolverines. The area is known for badly storms. Visit with a good trained guide.

If it is aquatic animals you really want to see, you should go to the Everglades in Florida. If you paddle good and are in well shape, you can canoe or kayak on the water trails. Visit in January or February, or you may be bad bitten by mosquitoes. Those who visit are really excited to see alligators, dolphins, crocodiles, flamingos, and manatees. From Alaska to Florida and many places in between, well wildlife viewing is there for you to see.

Try It
Write an article describing a school event in which some things went well, and some things didn't go so well. Use each of the words *bad, badly, good, well, really,* and *very* at least once.

Answers will vary.

121

Homophones are words that sound the same but have different spellings and different meanings. There are hundreds of homophones in the English language.

allowed: to be permitted   *aloud*: to be audible
buy: to purchase   *by*: to be near
main: the most important   *mane*: hair

If you are unsure about which homophone to use, look up the meanings in a dictionary.

Match It
Read the following sentences. Circle the letter of the definition of the underlined homophone that fits the sentence.

1. Taylor will have many books to <u>buy</u> when he starts college.
   (a.) to purchase
   b. to be near
2. The horse's <u>mane</u> glistened in the morning sunshine.
   a. the most important
   (b.) hair
3. My father said we weren't <u>allowed</u> to see that movie.
   (a.) to be permitted
   b. to be audible
4. Ellen lives <u>by</u> the pond with the ducks and geese.
   a. to purchase
   (b.) to be near
5. Please underline the sentence with the <u>main</u> idea in this paragraph.
   (a.) the most important
   b. hair
6. The students will recite the poems <u>aloud</u>.
   a. to be permitted
   (b.) to be audible

122

Spectrum Language Arts
Grade 5

Proof It
Proofread the story, and use proofreading marks to correct the homophones.

- deletes letters, words, punctuation
∧ - inserts letters, words, punctuation

More than anything, Luke wanted a horse for his birthday. He and his family lived on a farm, so why couldn't he have a horse to call his own? So far, he hadn't been ~~aloud~~ *allowed* to have his own horse. This year was going to be different. Luke's father said he could have a horse if he could ~~by~~ *buy* it himself. He would pay Luke for chores he did on the farm. Then, Luke could ~~by~~ *buy* the horse he wanted. For his birthday, Luke's parents would ~~by~~ *buy* all of the ~~mane~~ *main* supplies and equipment he would need. Luke liked this deal. Then, the horse would really belong to him. It would be his responsibility to feed, clean, and exercise his horse. Luke found the perfect horse at a stable ~~by~~ *by* their farm. He had beautiful brown hair and a shiny ~~main~~ *mane*. Luke was so excited he shouted ~~allowed~~ *aloud*, "Thank you for my wonderful present! He'll be my friend forever!" Luke was glad he wasn't ~~aloud~~ *allowed* to have a horse until now. He was more grown up now and could take good care of a horse himself. His horse whinnied ~~allowed~~ *aloud*. Luke smiled. It was a perfect birthday.

Try It
Write a sentence of your own for each of the six homophones from this lesson: *allowed, aloud, buy, by, main,* and *mane.*

Answers will vary.

123

Homophones are words that sound the same but have different spellings and different meanings. The homophones *passed* and *past, threw* and *through,* and *to* and *too* are often confused.

passed: went by	*past:* former
threw: tossed	*through:* finished
to: toward	*too:* also

Complete It
Complete the following sentences by circling the correct homophone in parentheses.

1. Today's lesson is about more than Presidents; it's about their pets, (to, **too**).
2. President Benjamin Harrison's grandchildren liked to hitch a small cart (**to**, too) the President's pet goat, His Whiskers, and ride around the White House lawn.
3. Once His Whiskers escaped (threw, **through**) an open gate.
4. The President ran after His Whiskers and led the goat and the children back (**to**, too) the White House.
5. President Lyndon B. Johnson was kind (**to**, too) a stray when his daughter Luci found a small mutt.
6. President Calvin Coolidge's raccoon, Rebecca, had her own house on White House grounds. He walked (**to**, too) her house every day and took her on a walk on a leash.
7. Not only did Luci Johnson adopt a stray, but Chelsea Clinton, daughter of President Bill Clinton, did, (to, **too**).
8. When Chelsea went (**to**, too) college, the president's secretary, Betty Currie, took in Socks the cat.
9. The pets of (passed, **past**) Presidents are quite popular with the public.
10. The pets are so popular that a museum, the Presidential Pet Museum near Washington D.C., is dedicated just (**to**, too) them.

124

Find It
Use a dictionary to look [Answers will vary slightly. Accept all reasonable answers.] Write their definitions on the lines provided.

1. ad: <u>advertisement</u>
   add: <u>addition</u>
2. bail: <u>throw water out</u>
   bale: <u>bundle</u>
3. board: <u>lumber</u>
   bored: <u>uninterested</u>
4. bough: <u>of a tree</u>
   bow: <u>of a ship</u>
5. capital: <u>money; city</u>
   capitol: <u>U.S. Congress building</u>
6. do: <u>shall</u>
   dew: <u>moisture</u>
   due: <u>owed</u>
7. fair: <u>honest; bazaar</u>
   fare: <u>cost of transportation</u>
8. feat: <u>accomplishment</u>
   feet: <u>plural of foot</u>
9. flew: <u>past tense of fly</u>
   flu: <u>influenza</u>
   flue: <u>shaft</u>
10. knight: <u>feudal warrior</u>
    night: <u>evening</u>

Try It
Choose six of the groups above. Write sentences for all twelve words.

Answers will vary.

125

An apostrophe is used to substitute letters in **contractions**.

To form a contraction with *am*, drop the *a* and add an apostrophe.
I am tired today. *I'm* tired today.

To form a contraction with *are*, drop the *a* and add an apostrophe.
They are going to the beach. *They're* going to the beach.

To form a contraction with *is* or *has*, add an apostrophe and keep only the *s*.
She is ready to go. *She's* ready to go.
What has John been doing? *What's* John been doing?

To form a contraction with *would* or *had*, add an apostrophe and keep only the *d*.
He would be able to do that. *He'd* be able to do that.
I had thought of that. *I'd* thought of that.

To form a contraction with *will*, drop the *wi* and add an apostrophe where the *wi* was.
We will get the work done tomorrow. *We'll* get the work done tomorrow.

To form a contraction with *not*, drop the *o* and add an apostrophe where the *o* was.
We should not go there right now. *We shouldn't* go there right now.

The contraction for *let us* is *let's*.
Let us go home. *Let's* go home.

Match It
Draw a line from Column A to the contraction that could be substituted in Column B.

Column A
1. I am going to the humane society to adopt a dog.
2. The humane society has many animals up for adoption; it is a great way to save animals.
3. These animals are strays, or they have been abandoned or turned in as unwanted.
4. They had many pure bred dogs last week.
5. The shelter workers work hard with the animals so they will be ready to go to a good home.
6. We are also going to look at the cats, rabbits, and ferrets; they all need homes.
7. I can not wait until I'm 16 and can volunteer to walk dogs.
8. Let us hurry! Our dog is waiting!

Column B
can't
I'm
it's
let's
they'd
they'll
they've
we're

126

127

Solve It
Add the apostrophe where it is needed in each word. Then, write the words the contractions stand for.

1. he's __he is or he has__
2. you're __you are__
3. weren't __were not__
4. should've __should have__
5. I'm __I am__
6. she'd __she would or she had__
7. we'll __we will__
8. let's __let us__
9. can't __can not__
10. you'll __you will__
11. might've __might have__
12. here's __here is__

Try It
Write a sentence for each of the 12 contractions above.

Answers will vary.

128

A **negative** sentence states the opposite. Negative words include: *not, no, never, nobody, nowhere, nothing, barely, hardly, scarcely,* and contractions containing the word *not.*

Double negatives occur when two negative words are used in the same sentence. Don't use double negatives; it will make your sentence positive again, and it is poor grammar.

Negative: We do *not* have any soup in the pantry.
Double negative: We do *not* have *no* soup in the pantry.

Negative: I have *nothing* to wear to the party this weekend.
Double negative: I *don't* have *nothing* to wear to the party this weekend.

Negative: Greg can *hardly* put weight on his leg since his knee operation.
Double negative: Greg *can't hardly* put weight on his leg since his knee operation.

Identify It
Identify which of the following sentences have double negatives by writing an **X** on the lines. Then, go back and correct the double negatives by crossing out one of the negatives or by changing the wording.

1. _____ The chef hardly uses any fat in his cooking.
2. __X__ I don't like ~~no~~ green peppers on my pizza.
3. __X__ I can barely see ~~nothing~~ *anything* in this fog.
4. _____ The instructions never say to use a hammer.
5. __X__ Nobody ~~hardly~~ showed up at the premier.
6. __X__ Nowhere does it say to ~~not~~ add butter.
7. __X__ Please do not assign ~~no~~ more homework.
8. _____ We can scarcely finish the work we have now.
9. __X__ They don't have ~~no~~ money left for the ride home.
10. _____ I want to go swimming on vacation, but not snorkeling.
11. __X__ He can't have ~~no~~ more cookies.
12. __X__ I don't want to go ~~nowhere~~ *anywhere* until I've finished my work.
13. __X__ She ~~barely~~ can find nothing without her glasses.
14. __X__ He can't ~~never~~ lift something that big.
15. _____ We won't plant these flowers until spring.

129

Rewrite It
As you rewrite the paragraph, correct the double negatives.

Firefighting is a brave and courageous job. If you can't imagine yourself not working hard, then this job isn't for you. Firefighters go through special training. They don't never take training lightly. Some trainees don't make it through this training. Firefighters must train in actual fires. They may find they don't like climbing no ladders that are so high. Some may find they aren't scarcely strong enough. The firefighters who graduate are ready for the job. They don't know nothing about what lies ahead, but they are trained and ready. Firefighters keep us, our pets, and our homes safe. Firefighting is a brave and courageous career to explore.

__Firefighting is a very brave and courageous job. If you can't imagine yourself not working hard, then this job isn't for you. Firefighters go through special training. They never take training lightly. Firefighters must wear special gear and use special equipment. It isn't easy to use the equipment. They spend many class hours learning about it and training with it. Firefighters must train in actual fires. Some trainees don't make it through this training. They may find they don't like climbing ladders that are so high. Some may find they aren't strong enough. These men and women should still be respected for going through the training; it's just not the job for them. The firefighters who graduate are ready for the job. They don't know anything about what lies ahead, but they are trained and ready. Firefighters keep us, our pets, and our homes safe. Firefighting is a brave and courageous career to explore.__

Try It
Write four negative sentences using each of the following words: *not, nobody, nowhere,* and *nothing.* Do not use double negatives.

Answers will vary.

130

Review: Verbs: *come, do, go, run, see, sit*

Putting It Together
Complete the following sentences by circling the correct verb tense in parentheses.

1. My mom and dad (came, (come)) to visit my school for every open house.
2. Members of the track team (ran, (run)) home from school instead of walking.
3. Mitch ((did), do) his homework before he ate dinner.
4. Lori and Darrin ((saw), see) last year's parade, but didn't make it this year.
5. They (go, (have gone)) to the festival since they were children.
6. The birds (sit, (have sat)) in their nest since early morning.
7. I ((do), had done) my chores when I first get home from school.
8. I can (saw, (see)) much better with my glasses than without.
9. Noah (go, (went)) with his mother to the store yesterday afternoon.
10. Last evening, I ((ran), run) three laps around the track before going home.
11. The rain (come, (had come)) in downpours throughout the night.
12. They (see, (had seen)) the nurse long before the doctor arrived.
13. LeeAnn and Robby like to (go, (went)) to the hockey games every weekend.
14. Mr. Baldwin (run, (had run)) the lawn mower many times before it quit working.
15. After she had left, the babysitter ((came), had come) back to pick up her bookbag.
16. Rosemary wanted Jeanine to (sat, (sit)) with her.
17. Mr. Walsh (do, (has done)) that kind of work for years.
18. Bill ((sat), sit) and waited patiently for the interview to start.
19. Thomas cannot get his dog to ((run), ran).
20. Do you remember the last time we (do, (did)) this hike?
21. Did you (saw, (see)) the Wimbledon matches on TV last weekend?
22. Syd (go, (went)) on a river rafting trip last year.
23. Barbara liked to (ran, (run)) and swim for exercise.
24. The cook yelled, "((Come), Came) and get it!"
25. Mark ((saw), see) three raccoons in his backyard.

Review: Adjectives: *big/bigger/biggest, light/lighter/lightest, more/most, good/better/best, bad/worse/worst*; Adjectives and Adverbs: *bad/badly, good/well, very and really*

Identify the correct use of adjectives and adverbs by circling the correct answer in parentheses.

1. Stephanie thought "The Wizard of Oz" was the (cute, (cutest)) play she had seen all year.
2. We have to climb over one ((big,) biggest) rock in order to pass the test.
3. That is the (bigger, (biggest)) mountain I've ever seen.
4. Clint makes ((more,) most) money mowing lawns than Perry does selling lemonade.
5. The ice storm we had last night was ((worse,) worst) than the one we had last year.
6. Going to the beach for vacation is a (good, (better)) idea than going to the mountains.
7. The blizzard brought the (more, (most)) snow I had ever seen.
8. Snow skiing is a ((good,) best) winter sport.
9. I think swimming in the lake in the winter is a ((bad,) badly) idea.
10. Lakeside is a ((good,) well) park for hiking and biking.

Review: Homophones: *allowed/aloud, buy/by, main/mane, passed/past, threw/through, to/too*; Contractions; Negatives and Double Negatives

Proofread the following sentences. Check for incorrect homophones, missing apostrophes, and double negatives.

| ⌐ ~ deletes letters, words, punctuation |
| ^ ~ inserts letters, words, punctuation |

1. Diane was ~~going~~ allowed to visit her friends after she finished her homework.
2. Lynn wants to buy earrings with the money she earns from shoveling snow.
3. Elise brushes her horse's mane every morning and every night.
4. Mr. and Mrs. Jones ~~past~~ passed the turn they were supposed to make into the school.
5. Andrew threw the football the farthest.
6. Amy wanted to go to the game, too.
7. What's the best way to get there?
8. They're going the wrong direction.

131

Notes